FRENCH
GCSE Grade Booster

S. J. Shaw

Schofield & Sims Ltd.

© **1991 Schofield & Sims Ltd.**

All rights reserved.
No part of this publication may be
reproduced, stored in a retrieval system, or
transmitted, in any form, or by any means,
electronic, mechanical, photocopying,
recording or otherwise, without the prior
permission of Schofield & Sims Ltd.

0 7217 4617 9

First printed 1991

Acknowledgements

The author and the publishers wish to
thank the following for permission to use
copyright material:

London East Anglian Group: p.110

Northern Examining Association
(Yorkshire & Humberside Regional
Examinations Board): p.111

Schofield & Sims Ltd.
Dogley Mill
Fenay Bridge
Huddersfield
HD8 0NQ
England

Typeset by Ocean, Leeds
Printed in Great Britain by the Alden Press, Oxford

Contents

	Introduction	4
1	**Self, Family and Friends**	5
2	**House and Home**	10
3	**Town and Countryside, Directions**	16
4	**Food and Drink, Cafés and Restaurants**	24
5	**Daily Routine, Leisure, Going Out**	30
6	**Holidays and Tourist Situations**	35
7	**Work, School, Study**	48
8	**Health and Accidents**	52
9	**Travel, Customs, At the Garage**	55
10	**Shopping, Banking and Post Office, Returns and Complaints**	64
11	**Structures Guide**	
	Section 1 – Verbs: Verb Agreement, Verb Tenses	69
	2 – Genders: Articles, Adjectives	88
	3 – Prepositions, Simple Prepositions, 'de' Prepositions, 'à' Prepositions	91
	4 – How to Make Questions	93
	5 – How to Make Negatives	94
	6 – Pronouns	96
	7 – Idioms	99
12	**Skills Guide**	
	Listening	102
	Speaking	104
	Reading + Examples	109
	Writing + Examples	112
	Appendices	
	Appendix 1 – Question words, Key phrases for rôle-play, Important time expressions	119
	2 – Numbers, cardinal and ordinal + dates	121
	3 – Time, digital and clock-face	124
	4 – Learning vocabulary	126
	5 – Practising interviews	128

Introduction

This book, as its name suggests, is designed to help you to boost your grade in GCSE French. It is intended:
- to help you to revise and to refresh your memory;
- to be easy, so that you can work through it on your own;
- to show you how to tackle the various sections of the examination;
- to help you to organise in your mind what you have already learnt;
- to help you to fill any gaps if you have missed anything during your course;
- to help you to show the examiner what you know (and improvise what you don't know).

It is *not* intended:
- to be a course book;
- to be a copy of any GCSE syllabus;
- to be a phrase-book or dictionary;
- to be difficult or complicated.

As the GCSE Examination Boards offer syllabuses which are basically similar, this book has been designed to cover the *core* requirements of all these syllabuses. It has been kept short to fit easily in your revision schedule.

The Format of the Book

The syllabuses for GCSE French are organised in topics. The first ten chapters in this book cover all the topics in the syllabuses, though they may vary in order. Each of the topics can be tested in some part of the examination; indeed, most topics will be tested in more than one part of the exam.

Certain topics require frequent use of particular language structures. A summary of the most important is included in the *Structures Guide*.

The GCSE examination tests your ability in French in each of the four skills – Listening, Reading, Speaking and Writing. The skills most likely to be tested in connection with each topic are indicated at the beginning of that chapter. Each skill requires a different set of techniques, and guide-lines for these techniques are given in the *Skills Guide*.

The Format of the Cassette

The cassette is divided into two sections:
SECTION 1 is designed to improve your speaking by:
- demonstrating typical interviews and/or rôle-plays for the 10 topic areas;
- giving examples of good technique;
- reminding you how to pronounce the material in your notes.

SECTION 2 is intended to help you 'tune in' your listening by focusing your attention on sample short items taken at random from Section 1.

▭ in the text indicates material recorded on the cassette.

1 Self, Family and Friends

In this chapter, you are going to cover the following:
Your relative or friend's name
Your relative or friend's age
Number of brothers and sisters
Physical appearance
Characteristics
Work
Interests and routine.

Describing People

Here is a simple letter you might write if you had been asked to find a pen-friend for your sister:

Brighton, le 9 octobre

Chère Isabelle,

Merci de ta dernière lettre. Comment ça va? Chez nous, tout le monde va bien. Est-ce que tu pourrais m'aider?

Ma soeur Julie - la plus jeune de la famille - a onze ans maintenant et elle va au collège avec moi. Elle apprend le français depuis six semaines et elle voudrait avoir une correspondante française. Est-ce que tu connais une fillette du même âge - une amie de ton frère, peut-être - qui voudrait bien écrire à ma soeur?

Elle a un peu plus d'onze ans, elle est mince et assez petite. Elle a les yeux bleus et les cheveux blonds, assez courts et bouclés. Elle est sportive : elle joue au tennis et au hockey - et elle est aussi assez intelligente!

Elle travaille bien au collège. Ses matières préférées sont le français et la musique - elle joue de la guitare. A la maison, elle écoute des disques - elle adore la musique pop - et elle regarde la télé. Le week-end, elle fait de l'équitation et elle aime beaucoup danser.

D'habitude, il y a une discothèque au club des jeunes et elle y va souvent. Maman dit qu'elle est paresseuse, parce qu'elle n'aime pas faire la vaisselle - moi non plus!

Describing People

> *Est-ce que tu as reçu les magazines que j'ai envoyés il y a quinze jours ?...*

This is the sort of information you may be expected to communicate in the Speaking or Writing Tests, referring either to yourself, or to a relative or a friend.

🔲 Listen to the model interview on the cassette. Marianne is describing herself and her brother, in response to these questions:

> *Comment t'appelles-tu?*
> *Tu as quel âge?*
> *Tu as des frères ou des soeurs?*
> *Comment s'appelle ton frère?*
> *Il a quel âge?*
> *Tu peux me décrire ton frère?*
> *Quels sont ses passe-temps préférés?*
> *Qu'est-ce qu'il fait d'habitude le week-end?*

To answer these questions, you can use the following in talking or writing:

Name

Je m'appelle	...
Il s'appelle	
Elle s'appelle	

Age

J'ai	...	ans
Il a		
Elle a		

Brothers and sisters

J'ai	un frère	
	deux frères	
	une soeur	
	deux soeurs	
Je suis	fils	unique
	fille	
	enfant	

Physical appearance

Je suis	très	grand(e)
Il est	assez	petit(e)
Elle est	plutôt	gros(se)
		mince

Describing People

Hair and eyes

J'ai Il a Elle a	*les yeux*			*bleus* *gris* etc.
	les cheveux	*blonds* *bruns*	*et*	*courts* *longs* *bouclés* *raides*

People and relationships

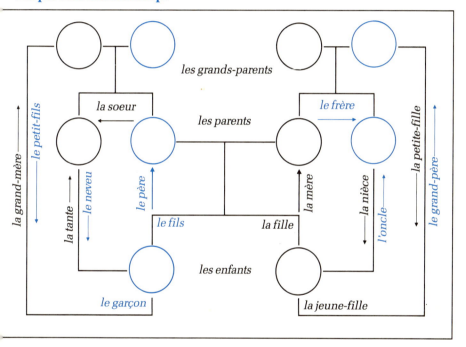

Characteristics

Je suis Il est Elle est	*aimable* *egoïste* *intelligent(e)* *paresseux(se)* *studieux(se)* *stupide* *sympathique*

Status

Je suis Il est Elle est	*célibataire* *marié(e)* *divorcé(e)* *veuf/veuve*

Describing People

Describing People

Work

Je suis Il est Elle est	étudiant /étudiante mécanicien /mécanicienne vendeur /vendeuse professeur coiffeur /coiffeuse

Je travaille Il travaille Elle travaille	dans un café dans une boulangerie dans un collège dans un salon de coiffure

● More of these in Chapter 7.

Interests

J'aime Il aime Elle aime	danser écouter de la musique faire du ski aller à la pêche jouer au tennis

Routine

Je me lève		
Je prends Il prend Elle prend	mon petit déjeuner	à ... heures
Je vais Il va Elle va	au collège au travail travailler	

Preparation

The above material forms an outline for most spoken or written tasks on this topic. Look at the patterns and make sure you collect any additional vocabulary you will need to describe yourself, your relatives, your friend(s).

Written Tasks You Might Be Set

1. Fill in a form giving your personal details for a club or pen-friend or friendship agency.
2. Write a short profile of a friend (or teacher) for a French school magazine.
3. Describe your family to your new pen-friend.

2 House and Home

In this chapter you are going to look at the following:
Where you live
What your home is like
What rooms there are
What a room is like.

Describing Home

Here is the kind of letter which a French girl might write to her English pen-friend. Read it carefully, because this is the sort of letter you might be asked to write.

> 50, rue Victor-Hugo
> MONTEREAU
> Le 25 juin 1992
>
> Chère Tracey,
>
> Depuis lundi, nous habitons la nouvelle maison! Elle est beaucoup plus grande, et elle est située à la campagne, à quatre kilomètres de Béziers. Nous avons un grand jardin avec une pelouse et un petit verger avec des pommiers.
>
> La maison est assez moderne — construite il y a douze ou treize ans. Il y a trois étages — rez-de-chaussée, premier étage et grenier. Mais il n'y a pas de cave! Il y a huit pièces : une salle de séjour, une petite salle à manger, une grande cuisine, trois chambres, une salle de bains, et un cabinet de toilette.
>
> Deux des chambres et la salle de bains sont au premier étage. Le cabinet de toilette est à côté de la cuisine, au rez-de-chaussée. Ma chambre, c'est la mansarde. Elle est immense! Il y a deux grandes fenêtres qui donnent sur le bois et les prés — où il y a trois chevaux! J'ai mon lit, une armoire, deux placards, une table avec une chaise, où je fais mes devoirs et...

What is the French girl telling Tracey? She is telling her about their new house, where it is, how it is different from their previous house, how old it is, what rooms there are, and about her own room.

Describing Home

🎧 Now listen to Michel being interviewed about the house where he lives. He is answering certain questions:

> *Où habites-tu?*
> *Comment est ta maison?*
> *Il y a combien d'étages?*
> *Combien de pièces y a-t-il?*
> *Où est ta chambre?*
> *Qu'est-ce qu'il y a dans ta chambre?*

To answer these questions, use the following in talking or writing:

Where you live

J'habite	à Béziers un appartement une maison

Il Elle	est	situé située	au centre-ville dans la banlieue à ... kilomètres de ... à la campagne
	se trouve		

What your home is like
Flat

C'est un	petit grand	appartement, qui est assez	moderne. vieux.

Il est situé au	premier deuxième	étage.

House

C'est une	petite grande	maison. Elle est assez	moderne. vieille.

Il y a ... étages.				
Il y a un	petit grand	jardin	devant derrière	la maison

Describing Home

What rooms there are

Il y a	... pièces une salle de séjour une salle à manger une cuisine un vestibule une chambre trois chambres une salle de bains un cabinet de toilette + un grenier une cave

Where the rooms are

Ma chambre est	dans le grenier sous le toit au deuxième étage au premier étage au rez-de-chaussée dans la cave

In relation to others

... près de la salle de bains ... à côté de la salle à manger ... en face de la cuisine, etc.

- Careful! If you want to say *en face de, près de,* etc. with a *le* word, you need *du*:
   e.g. *Près du vestibule*   *En face du vestibule*   etc.

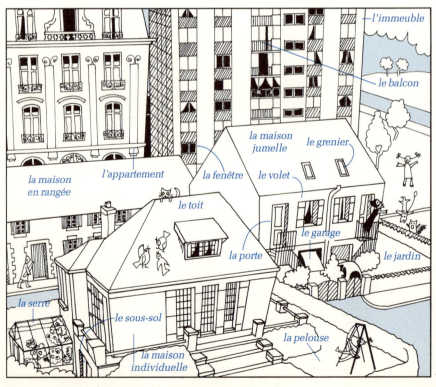

Describing Home

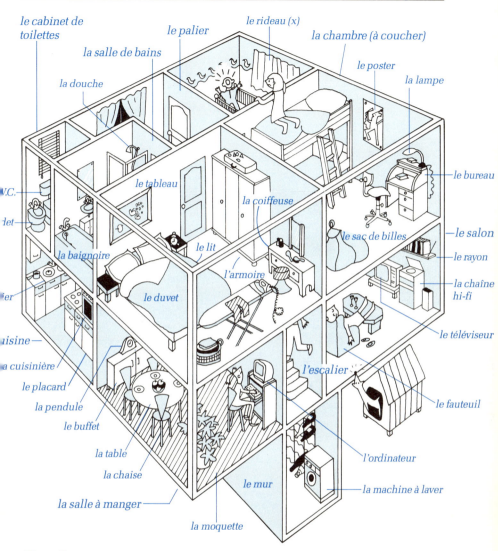

Size of room

Ma chambre La salle de séjour	est	très petite petite assez petite assez grande grande très grande immense

Describing Home

Colours of room

Les murs sont	blancs verts
Le tapis est	gris vert
La porte est	blanche verte, etc.

Outside the house or flat

Nous avons	un balcon . . . un jardin . . . un garage . . . une serre . . .

Contents of room

Il y a	une fenêtre deux fenêtres une table un fauteuil un lit un placard une commode un téléviseur . . . sur le placard

Where

. . . devant . . . derrière	la maison

- Under this topic, you could also be asked to talk about what you do in a certain room. For this information, please see Chapter 5: Routine and Leisure.

Describing Home

Preparation

First, look at your vocabulary lists. Do you have all the items of vocabulary you need to use to talk about your home? Or your friends' homes? The answer is probably 'No'. Set to work now to collect the rest of the vocabulary and phrases you will need, from your old vocabulary books or your dictionary. You should certainly include colours, extra rooms and furniture under this topic.

🖭 Now that you have worked through some of the basic materials, listen to Oral Tests A and B on the tape. Both candidates are being interviewed about their homes. What difference do you notice between them? Which do you think is the better 'performance'? Why does one candidate get the chance to say more?

If you have prepared your material well, your examiner will be able to give you the opportunity to discuss your home, asking questions to help you develop your ideas.

- Remember, prepare your material so that you can give full answers. Do not learn a speech and try to recite it: the examiner will soon spot what you are doing and cut you off.
- Do listen to the questions – they do not always come in the order you expect!

Written Tasks You Might Be Set

1. Imagine you have just moved to a new house. Write a postcard to your French pen-friend, giving your address and saying where your house is situated and what it is like.

2. Imagine that you are staying in a holiday flat, in England or abroad. Write a postcard to your French pen-friend describing the flat, saying which floor it is on and what rooms there are.

3. Imagine that you are going to exchange homes with a French family for the summer holidays. Write an advertisement in simple French to say what your house is like and what facilities there are.

4. Write a letter to your French pen-friend describing what rooms there are in your house, and in particular what your room is like, before s/he comes to visit you.

3 Town and Countryside, Directions

In this chapter, you are going to cover the following:
Where you live/where a friend lives
Where your town or village is situated
What it is like
What buildings or other places there are
Where certain buildings are
What facilities there are and what you can do
Your opinion of this town or village, with reasons.

Town

Here is a simple description of a 'typical' French town:

> Bonville se trouve dans le nord-est de la France. C'est une petite ville industrielle mais pittoresque, de 15000 habitants. Le centre même est assez moderne, construit il y a vingt ans, mais autour du centre-ville, il y a de vieux bâtiments très intéressants.
>
> A Bonville, il y a beaucoup de magasins, deux églises, deux écoles primaires et un CES*, quelques cafés, une piscine, un stade, un joli jardin public avec un court de tennis, un petit musée d'horloges et un cinéma.
>
> La plupart des magasins se trouvent sur la Place du Marché. On y trouve aussi la poste, qui est située à côté de l'Hôtel de Ville et, en face de la poste, il y a un petit supermarché. Malheureusement, il n'y a pas d'hypermarché. Pour cela, il faut aller à Rouen. Il y a le marché trois fois par semaine, le mardi, le vendredi et le samedi.
>
> La gare se trouve tout près, à 200 mètres, dans la rue de la République, près de la bibliothèque. La gare routière est en face du Musée d'Horloges.
>
> Il y a beaucoup de choses à faire pour s'amuser: on peut nager ou jouer au tennis, se promener dans le jardin public, prendre un verre de vin dans un café

> ou visiter le musée, qui est ouvert tous les jours.
> Pour les jeunes, il y a aussi une disco et un club de jeunes.
>
> *CES: Collège d'Enseignement Secondaire

Where is the town situated? What is it like? How old is it? What is there in Bonville? Where exactly is the post office? Where is the bus station? What leisure facilities are there, or what is there to do in one's leisure time?

We are told:

- that it is in the north-east of France;
- that it is industrial but quite pleasant;
- that the town centre is quite modern, with interesting older buildings nearby;
- that there are plenty of shops, three schools, cafés, a swimming-pool, a sports stadium, a park with tennis court, etc.;
- that the post office is in the market square, next to the town hall;
- that the bus station is opposite the Clock Museum;
- in one's leisure time, one can swim, play tennis, walk, go to one of the cafés, visit the museum or go to a disco, or youth club.

This is the sort of information you will be expected to give in the Speaking or Writing Tests.

Listen to Sylvie being interviewed about where she lives. She is responding to these questions:

> *Où habites-tu?*
> *Où se trouve Tours-les-Bains?*
> *C'est un village?*
> *Qu'est-ce qu'il y a à Tours-les-Bains?*
> *Tu peux me décrire le centre-ville?*
> *Qu'est-ce qu'on peut faire à Tours-les-Bains?*
> *Tu aimes habiter à Tours-les-Bains?*
> *Pourquoi?*

Town

To answer these questions, you can use the following in talking or writing:

Where you live/a friend lives

J' Mon ami Mon amie	habite à ...

What buildings there are

Il y a	un musée une cathédrale des cafés quelques églises

Where it is situated

...	se trouve est	dans le au	nord nord-ouest sud	de l'Angleterre de la Belgique de la France*

*France only: *dans le / au Sud* = *dans le Midi* (the South of France).

What it is like

C'est	un petit(e) village une grand(e) ville	industriel(le) rural(e) pittoresque touristique

C'est un village/une ville industriel(le)/assez important(e)

Where the buildings are

Le musée La cathédrale	se trouve est situé(e)	près du/de la ... à côté du/de la ... en face du/de la ...
Les cafés Les deux églises	se trouvent sont situé(e)s	sur le/la ... dans le/la ...

Facilities and what there is to do

Either:

On peut	jouer au football nager faire de l'équitation faire des achats se promener

Or:

Pour les jeunes, il y a	un club une discothèque etc.

Town

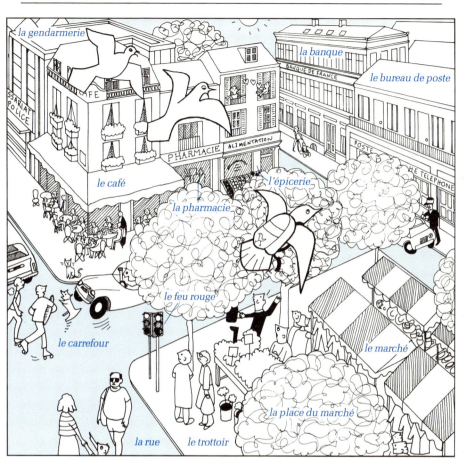

Your opinion

J'aime ... (town)	
Je n'aime pas ... (town)	

Je l'aime bien
Je ne l'aime pas du tout
Je le déteste

Je préfère ... (town)
Je préférerais habiter à ... (town)

The reasons

Parce que c'est	agréable
	ennuyeux

Parce qu'il y a beaucoup de choses à faire
Parce qu'il n'y a rien à faire

Countryside

If you live in the country, it is easy to adapt the town pattern.

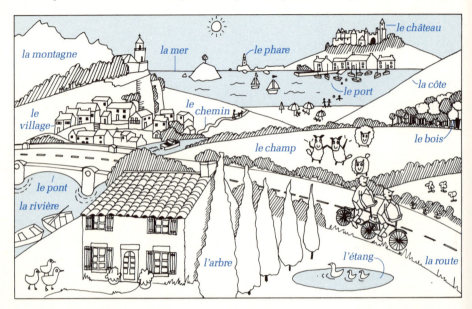

Here is an extract from a letter describing a day out in the country:

> Il faisait si beau et nous avons décidé de faire un pique-nique à la campagne. Nous connaissons un petit endroit près de la rivière qui est très joli. D'un côté, il y a des prés où on voit souvent quelques chevaux (ce qui plaît beaucoup aux enfants), et de l'autre côté, il y a des bois. Si on traverse le petit pont, on peut faire une longue promenade dans les bois. Si on préfère, on peut marcher le long de la rivière jusqu'au petit lac, où on peut aller à la pêche.
> Et nous ? Nous sommes restés près du pont, pendant que les enfants jouaient dans l'eau.

This extract shows several of the phrases you could use if asked about the countryside. The vocabulary is different, but the basic structures are similar.

e.g. *il y a des près ... des bois.*
... on peut faire une longue promenade.

Preparation

The above material forms the basis for most tasks likely to be set for this topic.

First, look at the patterns and make sure you collect the vocabulary you will need in order to talk or write about your town etc., plus a typical French town or village. Think of the main activities you can do and list the verbs to describe them.

🎦 Now that you have prepared your basic material, listen to Oral Tests A and B on the tape. Both candidates are being interviewed about their town. What is the main difference between them? How much do the candidates say? Think about these before reading on.

Apart from Karen's initial blunder (you must listen carefully to every question, even the first!), neither candidate says anything wrong. Yet compare how much less the examiner needs to say in the second interview, and how much more the second candidate says.

Your examiner will try to make the interview as natural a conversation as possible, but if you do not respond fully to the questions and prompts, then he or she has to say more to help you, and you say less! This is not good news, because it goes without saying that you are being assessed on the degree to which you can communicate.

Written Tasks You Might Be Set

1. Write a postcard to your French pen-friend, describing the village where you are holidaying in England. Say where it is, what features there are and what there is to do.
2. Your pen-friend has written to ask you about your town. You send her a town plan with the main buildings marked (this would be supplied in the exam) and describe the main features and what one can do.

Directions

🎦 Listen to the model dialogue on the cassette. You can hear a tourist asking directions, and checking them.

Asking, or giving, directions is frequently set as a GCSE task in the Speaking Test. Overleaf are some of the key phrases you would need.

Directions

Getting attention

Pardon,	monsieur. madame. mademoiselle.	Je suis	étranger. étrangère.	Vous pouvez m'aider?

Asking

Il y a (un supermarché) près d'ici? *Où se trouve (le commissariat de police)?* *Je voudrais aller (à la gare). C'est loin d'ici?*	
Pour aller	*(au syndicat d'initiative)?* *(à la gare routière)?*

Directing

(To a friend)
  Continue
(To a stranger)
  Continuez
	tout droit . . .

. . . jusqu'	*au feu rouge* *à la place . . .*

Traverse *Traversez*	*la place* *la rue*

Tourne *Tournez*	*à gauche* *à droite*

Prends *Prenez*	*la*	*première* *deuxième* *troisième*	*rue*	*à gauche* *à droite*

Tu arriveras *Vous arriverez*	*à . . .*

Tu trouveras *Vous trouverez*	*. . .*	*à gauche* *à droite*	or	*sur*	*ta* *votre*	*gauche* *droite*

Checking

Alors,	*je continue . . .* *je traverse . . .* *je tourne . . .* *je prends . . .*	and	*j'arriverai . . .* *je trouverai . . .*

C'est loin d'ici? *C'est à quelle distance d'ici?*

Thanking

Merci bien, monsieur / madame / mademoiselle.
Merci mille fois, monsieur, etc.

Rôle-plays

Here are two examples of the sort of task you might be set in the Speaking Test. Look at the way each task is set out, then listen to an example of each rôle-play on the cassette.
- Remember to be polite always. Use *monsieur, madame, s'il vous plaît,* etc.

1. You are in a French town and stop a passer-by.
   1 – Ask if there is a tourist office there.
   2 – Ask how to get there.
   3 – Find out if it is far.

2. You are out shopping in your home town when a French tourist asks if you can help him. He wants to get to the bus station.
   1 – Tell him to go straight on to the traffic-lights.
   2 – Tell him to turn right, then left.
   3 – Correct his mistake.
   4 – Tell him it's 400 metres away.
   5 – Say it's a pleasure.

When you have heard them a couple of times, play them again, this time taking the parts of the tourist and passer-by yourself.
- Remember, the task often looks much more complicated than it is. Do not attempt to translate word for word. Think of the French you know which will convey the meaning or message required.
- Throughout the book, once you are used to what is required, try taking part in the rôle-plays.

Food and Drink

4 Food and Drink, Cafés and Restaurants

In this chapter, you are going to cover the following:
  Saying when and where you have meals
  Saying when you normally eat
  Saying what you ate at a particular meal
  Describing a picnic or a visit to a restaurant
  Ordering food and drink
  Discussing the order with a friend
  Complaining.

Food and Drink

Listen to the model interview with the boy on the cassette. Jean-Paul is responding to these questions:

> *A quelle heure est-ce que tu prends le petit déjeuner d'habitude?*
>
> *Où est-ce que tu prends le petit déjeuner?*
>
> *Qu'est-ce que tu manges au petit déjeuner?*
>
> *Qu'est-ce que tu aimes boire?*
>
> *Hier soir, qu'est-ce que tu as mangé au dîner?*
>
> *Est-ce que tu vas faire un pique-nique quelquefois?*
>
> *Quelle était la dernière fois que vous avez fait un pique-nique?*
>
> *Tes copains et toi, qu'est-ce que vous avez mangé?*
> *Qu'est que vous avez bu?*
>
> *Qui a préparé le pique-nique?*

To answer these questions, you can use the following in talking:

When you have meals

Je prends *On prend* *Nous prenons*	*le petit déjeuner* *le déjeuner* *le goûter* *le dîner* *un casse-croûte*	*à . . . heures (et demie)*

Food and Drink

Also:

Je On	déjeune . . .
Nous déjeunons . . .	

Je On	dîne . . .
Nous dînons . . .	

Je On	goûte . . .
Nous goûtons . . .	

Where you have meals

Je prends On prend Nous prenons	le petit déjeuner le déjeuner le goûter le dîner	dans la cuisine dans la salle à manger dans ma chambre au collège

Also:

Je	déjeune dîne mange	dans . . . à la/au . . .

What you eat or drink for . . .

D'habitude	je mange	une tartine du poulet des frites	au petit déjeuner au déjeuner
	je bois	un verre de coca une tasse de café	au dîner

What you like to eat or drink

J'aime	(bien) (beaucoup)	manger	le poulet les gâteaux
		boire	le café le chocolat au lait

What you or (the) others ate or drank

J' Mon frère Ma mère	ai a a	mangé	une pizza de la salade du fromage
J' Mon père Ma soeur	ai a a	bu	une boîte de coca de la limonade une bière, etc.

Food and Drink

When you last (went out)

C'était	en été le jour de mon anniversaire il y a quinze jours

- *Il y a* + time = ago.

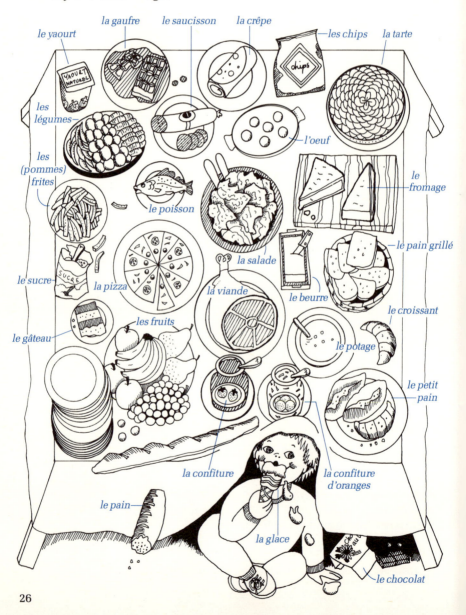

Cafés and Restaurants

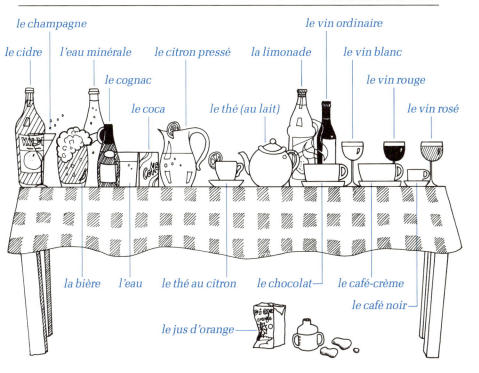

Preparation

These expressions give you the basic framework for talking or writing about eating and drinking. You need to make sure that you know a reasonable range (at least five or six of each) of breakfast items, snacks, café foods, main dishes, vegetables, fruits, and hot and cold drinks.

Cafés and Restaurants

Here are some of the basic phrases and structures you will need.

Booking or getting a table

Je voudrais (réserver) Est-ce que vous avez	une table pour . . . personnes (?)

Getting the menu, wine list, etc.

Garçon! Mademoiselle!	Je voudrais Donnez-moi	la carte la carte des vins	s'il vous plaît

Ordering

Je voudrais	le menu à soixante-quinze francs
Je vais prendre Nous voudrions	des escargots un bifteck (bien cuit) une bouteille de ...

Rejecting

Je Mon ami Mon amie	ne mange pas	de	frites viande salade champignons porc
Je Mon ami Mon amie	ne veut pas		
Je Mon ami Mon amie	n'aime pas		les frites la viande la salade les champignons le porc

Requesting

Est-ce que	je peux		avoir	des pommes de terre? du poisson? du boeuf?
Est-ce qu'	il elle	peut		

Discussing what to order (with a friend)

Tu as	soif? faim?
Tu veux manger tout de suite?	
Qu'est-ce que tu	manges? bois? prends (comme boisson)? peux me recommander?

Paying

L'addition Ça fait combien	s'il vous plaît (?)

- *Le service est compris?* = Is service included?

Complaining

Waiting

J'attends depuis un quart d'heure Je voudrais commander …

No fork, etc.

Je n'ai pas de	fourchette couteau cuillère

Wrong Order

J'ai commandé du poulet, ça, c'est du boeuf!

Food cold

Mon potage est froid

Food over-cooked

Mon bifteck est trop cuit

Choosing and Ordering a Meal

Listen to the two model dialogues: discussing what to order, and giving the order which has been discussed.

Rôle-play

Look at the following example of a rôle-play task which might be set on this topic:

> You are in a restaurant in France with your girl/boyfriend who can speak no French.
>
> 1 – Order onion soup for both of you.
> 2 – Say your friend would like chicken, chips and salad.
> 3 – Say you would like chicken as well, but check if you can have green beans instead of chips.

As you can hear, there is no need to translate the exact wording of the task.

Routine

5 Daily Routine, Leisure, Going Out

In this chapter, you are going to deal with your usual routine or leisure activities in the present tense, including:

Getting up and going to bed
Mealtimes
Your morning routine
Your activities at home
Helping
Going out with friends.

Routine

🔲 Listen to the model interview, number 1 on the tape. Marcel is talking about how he spends a typical Saturday. He is responding to these questions:

> *A quelle heure te lèves-tu d'habitude le samedi?*
> *A quelle heure prends-tu le petit déjeuner?*
> *Qu'est-ce que tu fais avant de manger?*
> *Est-ce que tu sors le samedi matin?*
> *Qu'est-ce que tu fais à la maison?*
> *Et l'après-midi?*
> *Quand est-ce que tu rentres à la maison?*
> *Et après le dîner?*
> *Tu te couches de bonne heure le samedi?   Pourquoi pas?*

Bedtimes and mealtimes form a useful framework. To talk or write about these, you can use the following:

Bedtimes and mealtimes

	je me lève	à sept heures et demie
D'habitude	je prends le petit déjeuner* je déjeune* je dîne*	à neuf heures à midi à six heures
	je me couche	à dix heures et demie

Routine

*or:

D'habitude	le matin, à midi, je mange le soir,	...

Morning routine

Je me douche Je prends ma douche		à huit heures
Je me lave	les cheveux la tête	sous la douche
Je m'habille Je me peigne		dans ma chambre dans la salle de bains

Home-based activities

Je regarde la télévision		
J'écoute	mes	disques cassettes
	la radio	
Je lis	un livre des magazines	
Je fais	mes devoirs dans ma chambre	
Je joue	aux cartes avec ma soeur	
Je joue	au football dans le jardin	
Je joue	avec mon chien, etc.	

Helping

Je fais	mon lit	
Je range	mes affaires dans ma chambre	
Je prépare	le déjeuner	
Je lave	la vaisselle	
Je fais	les courses des achats	pour ma mère
Je passe	l'aspirateur	
J'aide	ma grand-mère dans la cuisine mon frère dans le jardin	

Going out (with friends)

Je vais en ville Je vais chez mon ami(e) Je vais au match de football		avec	mon ami(e) mon chien mes ami(e)s mon frère ma soeur
Je vais	à la discothèque au cinéma à la piscine au club des jeunes		
Je fais une promenade Je vais me promener Je me promène			
Je vais à la pêche			

Now listen to the model interview, number 2 on the tape. Madeleine is talking about how she spent <u>last</u> Sunday. The questions are similar to Marcel's, but are in the past perfect tense, so she must answer in the past perfect.

> Qu'est-ce que tu <u>as</u> <u>fait</u> dimanche dernier?
> Tu <u>as</u> <u>mangé</u> à quelle heure?
> Tu <u>es</u> encore <u>sortie</u>?
> Tu t'<u>es</u> <u>couchée</u> à quelle heure?
> Pourquoi?

Preparation

Now you must 'collect' the sentences to describe your activities or routine: first in the present (one verb-word tense), then in the past perfect (two verb-words).

Remember:
- A reflexive verb, such as *je me lève*, becomes *je me <u>suis</u> <u>levé(e)</u>*.
- One of the 'group of 13 verbs', such as *je vais*, becomes *je <u>suis</u> <u>allé(e)</u>*.
- One of the other verbs, such as *j'écoute*, becomes *j'<u>ai</u> <u>écouté</u>*.

You may also be asked to talk or write about activities you plan for <u>next</u> weekend, etc. For this, it is best to use the 'future with *aller*'.

Routine

The questions will sound like these:

> *Qu'est-ce que tu <u>vas</u> <u>faire</u> samedi prochain?*
> *Tu <u>vas</u> <u>sortir</u>?*
> *Tu <u>vas</u> <u>rester</u> à la maison?*

Your answers should begin *'Je vais . . .'*

Written Tasks You Might Be Set

1. Imagine your French pen-friend will be staying with you for the weekend. Write, describing your <u>normal</u> routine, so that he or she knows what to expect. This may include other members of the family, too.
2. You may be asked to write about what you will do together, when your pen-friend arrives. This will involve 'we'.
3. You may well be asked to write about how you spent a boring weekend at home – or an exciting birthday weekend!

It is important that you read the task outline carefully, and decide whether it is to be your normal activities (present), looking ahead (future), or looking back to what happened earlier (past perfect).

You may well be required to do two sections about two different time periods and will need a different tense in each.

- What you must <u>not</u> do is 'drift' from one tense to another!

Holidays

Holidays and Tourist Situations

This is one of the most extensive topics and can range from talking or writing about leisure activities, when people are simply on holiday from school or work, to a discussion or an account of a particular holiday trip at home or abroad. It also includes booking accommodation and getting help or information from tourist and lost property offices.

Activities When Not at Work or at School

This topic will normally be discussed in the present tense (one verb-word) and will include many of the phrases used in Chapter 5. Questions will be on the lines of:

> *Qu'est-ce que tu <u>fais</u> d'habitude quand tu <u>as</u> congé?*
>
> *Comment est-ce que tu <u>passes</u> les vacances de Pâques?*
>
> *Tu peux me raconter* { *comment tu <u>passes</u>* / *ce que tu <u>fais</u> pendant* } *les grandes vacances?*

● It is important to listen for key verbs such as *passes* or *fais* in the present tense, or the helpful *d'habitude* (= usually), to check which tense to respond in.

You can use a whole range of ideas from Chapter 5, but you may want to add such ideas as:

Staying at home

Je reste à la maison

Working

Je travaille dans ...
Je travaille comme ...

Visiting

Je rends visite à ...

Going for walk

Je me promène
Je fais une promenade

Going for a picnic

Je	fais un / vais en	pique-nique

Going for a trip

Je fais une excursion

Baby-sitting

Je garde les enfants

With friends

... avec / ... chez	mes amis

35

Shopping

Je fais	les courses
	des achats

Sun-bathing

Je me fais bronzer	sur la plage
	dans le jardin

Particular Holiday Trip (Past)

Listen to the interview on the cassette. Isabelle is being questioned about her recent holiday in Carnac.

She is asked these questions:

> Tu <u>es allée</u> en vacances l'été dernier?
> Où est-ce que tu <u>es allée</u>?
> Tu y <u>es allée</u> avec des amis?
> Et le voyage à Carnac, c'<u>était</u> comment?
> Combien de temps est-ce que vous <u>avez passé</u> à Carnac?
> (= 'you' plural)
> Où est-ce que vous <u>avez logé</u>?
> L'hôtel <u>était</u> bien?
> Il y <u>avait</u> combien de chambres?
> Comment <u>était</u> ta chambre?
> Il y <u>avait</u> un restaurant?
> Où est-ce que vous <u>avez mangé</u> a midi?
> Qu'est-ce que vous <u>avez fait</u> pendant la journée?
> Et le soir ? Comment <u>avez-vous passé</u> le soir?
> Il <u>faisait</u> beau (temps)?

Notice that some of the questions are in the <u>past perfect</u> tense, using two verb-words, while some others are in the <u>past imperfect</u>, using one verb-word.

When you answer about what you <u>did</u>, you will need the <u>past perfect</u>.

I	We
J'ai (passé) ...	Nous avons (passé) ...
Je suis (allé(e)) ...	Nous sommes (allé(e)s) ...
Je me suis (couché(e)) ...	Nous nous sommes (couché(e)s) ...

Holidays

If you answer about what it was like, you will need the past imperfect:
C'était (petit)   Il y avait (une piscine)   Il faisait (chaud)
Il pleuvait

So to talk or write about your holiday you can use:

Where you went

Je suis allé(e)	à Bordeaux en France au bord de la mer à la campagne à la montagne

How long you stayed

J'ai passé	la journée le week-end la semaine quinze jours	à . . . en . . .

Who you went with

Je suis allé(e)	à . . . en . . . avec	ma famille ma soeur mon frère mes ami(e)s mon ami(e)

Where you stayed

J'ai Nous avons	logé	à l'hôtel dans une villa dans un gîte dans une caravane

What . . . was like

C'était	bien très bien	
	assez	petit grand moderne

What facilities there were

Il y avait	soixante chambres une piscine une discothèque un terrain de jeux un bon restaurant

The journey

Le voyage	était	bien long ennuyeux
	a duré six heures	

Holidays

Holidays

Where you ate

J'ai / Nous avons	pris	le déjeuner / le dîner	au restaurant / dans un café
Nous avons fait un pique-nique			sur la plage / dans les bois

What you did

J'ai / Nous avons	nagé	dans la piscine / dans la mer
	joué sur la plage	
	fait une promenade	
	visité	un château / un musée
	regardé	les vitrines / les devantures

Je suis / Nous sommes	allé(e) / allé(e)s	à Lyons / au zoo / à la mer / en ville
Je suis / Nous sommes	monté(e) / monté(e)s	en haut de la tour

Your evenings

J'ai / Nous avons	regardé la télé
	écouté de la musique
	dansé à la disco
	bavardé dans un café

Je suis / Nous sommes	allé(e) / allé(e)s	à la disco / au cinéma / au restaurant
	resté(e) / resté(e)s	à l'hôtel / sur le balcon

Holidays

The weather

Il faisait	beau mauvais froid chaud

Il y avait	du soleil du vent du brouillard
Il pleuvait Il neigeait	

As in other chapters, this is an <u>outline</u> for you to extend to describe <u>your</u> holiday activities.

Plans for Your Next Holiday

If you are asked to talk or write about your plans, you will need a future tense. It is easier (particularly if this is in your 'oral') to use the 'future with *aller*' (*futur composé*).

You will be describing many of the activities outlined above, but in the future. For example:

Je vais Nous allons	aller passer quinze jours	à Bournemouth en France
	loger dans un gîte aller en pique-nique manger dans un café jouer sur la plage visiter le château danser à la discothèque	

Because all the verbs operate to one pattern, future plans are easy to discuss. However, you still need to prepare the ideas, have the vocabulary ready and say what you are <u>probably</u> going to do, if you are asked:

Comment est-ce que tu vas passer les vacances?

or

Qu'est-ce que tu vas faire pendant les grandes vacances?

With the best will in the world, the examiner cannot give you many marks for *'Je ne sais pas'*!

In this chapter, there are also several important dialogues and rôle-plays involving information and accommodation. Here in the next few sections are the essential phrases.

At a Tourist Office *(Au syndicat d'initiative)*

🔲 Listen to the model dialogue, number 1 on the cassette. A tourist is asking for information.

Here are some of the most useful expressions:

Asking for help/information

Est-ce que vous pourriez m'aider,	
J'ai besoin de renseignements,	*s'il vous plaît (?)*
Je voudrais des informations,	

Things to ask for

Je voudrais *Avez-vous*	*un plan de la ville (?)* *une liste des hôtels (des campings) (?)* *des brochures (des dépliants) de . . . (?)* *des renseignements sur les excursions (?)* *un horaire des trains (des autobus) (?)*

Is there a . . . ?

Est-ce qu'il y a	*un camping* *une auberge de jeunesse* *une piscine* *un supermarché* *un bureau de change*	*près d'ici?*

Where is . . . ?

Où se trouve(nt)	*le bureau de poste?* *le marché?* *les magasins?* *la gare routière?*

Miscellaneous

Je vous dois combien?	How much do I owe you?
C'est gratuit?	Is it free of charge?
C'est ouvert tous les jours?	Is it open daily?
C'est fermé le dimanche?	Is it closed on Sundays?

Tourist Situations

At a Hotel *(A l'hôtel)*

Here are the key expressions:

Booking

Est-ce que vous avez une chambre de libre?
Je voudrais réserver une chambre . . .
J'ai réservé . . .

Type of room

Je voudrais	une chambre à un lit une chambre avec { un lit à deux personnes / un grand lit } une chambre à deux lits
	une chambre avec douche une chambre avec salle de bains
	une chambre qui donne sur le jardin une chambre qui donne sur la mer

Length of stay

C'est	pour une nuit pour aujourd'hui pour une semaine pour quinze jours

Costs

C'est combien par jour?	
C'est combien (par jour/semaine)	la demi-pension? la pension complète?
Le petit déjeuner est compris?	

Location

Où se trouve(nt)	ma chambre? l'ascenseur? les toilettes?

Miscellaneous

Pourriez-vous me donner ma clé, s'il vous plaît? My key, please. *Je voudrais la note (l'addition), s'il vous plaît.* My bill, please.		
J'arriverai *Nous arriverons*	*vers . . .*	I/We shall be arriving about . . .
Je partirai *Nous partirons*	*à . . .*	I/We shall be leaving at . . .
Je vais prendre la chambre. I'll take the room.		

At a Youth Hostel *(Dans une auberge de jeunesse)*

Here is a list of the most useful expressions:

Accommodation

Vous avez encore de la place?
Est-ce que vous avez des lits de libre pour aujourd'hui?

Location

Où se trouve le dortoir		*des garçons?* *des filles?*
Où est	*le père* *la mère*	*aubergiste, s'il vous plaît?*

Miscellaneous

Est-ce qu'on peut louer un sac de couchage?	Can you hire a sleeping-bag?
Est-ce qu'on peut dîner?	Can you have dinner (= evening meal)?
Le petit déjeuner est à quelle heure?	What time is breakfast?

At a Camp-site *(Au (terrain de) camping)*

Listen to the model dialogue, number 2 on the cassette. A tourist is booking a site for her caravan and awning.

Overleaf are some of the key expressions you may need:

Checking in

Où est	le gardien la gardienne	, s'il vous plaît?
Vous avez encore de la place?		
Nous avons	une tente deux tentes une caravane	
Il y a	deux adultes deux enfants un enfant	de ... ans
C'est combien	par nuit? par tente? par personne?	

Location
Where is (are) ... ?

Où se trouve(nt)	l'eau potable? les poubelles? les douches? les toilettes? le supermarché?

(Where) can you ... ?

	acheter	du pain? du lait?
	faire la lessive?	
(Où) est-ce qu'on peut	garer la voiture?	
	camper dresser la tente	(ici)?
	louer un vélo?	

When ... is open

Le supermarché La piscine	est ouvert(e) à quelle heure?

Tourist Situations

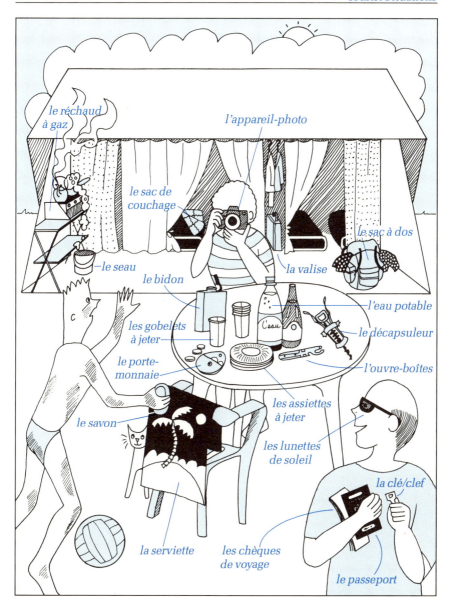

At the Lost-property Office

🎧 Listen to the model dialogue, number 3 on the cassette. It demonstrates how to enquire about a lost handbag.

Tourist Situations

Here are the essential expressions for reporting lost property. To <u>find</u> the lost-property office, you can say:

Pardon! Où se trouve le bureau des objets trouvés?

Say what you have lost

J'ai perdu	mon passeport ma valise mon porte-monnaie mon appareil-photo mon sac à main mon parapluie ma montre

Describe it

C'est		une Rolex/Canon	– to say the make
Il Elle	est	assez petit(e)/grand(e) en or/cuir/argent bleu foncé/noir(e)	– to say the size – to say the material – to say the colour

Say where you lost it

Je ne sais pas!	
Je l'ai perdu(e)	à la gare dans l'autobus dans la rue dans le parc

Say when you lost it

Je l'ai perdu(e)	ce matin hier vers dix heures entre midi et deux heures

Ask what to do

Qu'est-ce qu'il faut faire? Je dois revenir plus tard? Je dois téléphoner? Je dois attendre?

Miscellaneous

On a form *(une fiche),* you may be asked for personal details, e.g. name:

Je m'appelle . . . (family name first!)

and address:

J'habite (address in France!)   *numéro . . . , rue (de) . . .*
or phone number:
   C'est trente-cinq, dix, vingt-trois (35 10 23).
You may be asked to spell details such as name, street, etc, (in French). For how to say letters, listen to the short revision section at the end of the tape. Finally, you may want to offer a reward! Say:
   J'offre une récompense de . . . francs.

Rôle-plays

Here are two examples of rôle-play tasks you might be set. Study the wording of these as you listen to them on the tape.

---
1. You have arrived in a French town and need to find accommodation for your family for the night.
   - *1* – Ask if there are any rooms available.
   - *2* – Give details of two rooms you require.
   - *3* – Find out which floor they are on.
   - *4* – Check if breakfast is included.

---
2. You are on holiday in France and discover you have lost your camera. You go to the lost property office to ask for help.
   - *1* – Report that you have lost your camera.
   - *2* – Describe the camera.
   - *3* – Say when you lost it (this morning about 11 o'clock).
   - *4* – Ask if you should come back.

Written Tasks You May Be Set

1. Write a postcard to a French friend describing a day out at the coast.
2. Write a letter telling your French friend about a week of your holiday (at home or away) based on a diary, giving details of weather, what you did, what you enjoyed, etc.
3. Write a postcard from the camp-site where you are staying, describing the facilities and your plans for your stay.
4. Write a letter to a tourist information office in France, requesting information on a given town and a list of hotels (see Skills Guide).
5. Write a letter to a hotel manager or camp-site warden booking a room or site for one week for your family. Give dates, and say when you will be arriving (see Skills Guide).

7 Work, School, Study

In this chapter you will cover:
Talking about someone's job
Describing a day at work
Describing a school
Describing a school day
Talking about subjects and likes/dislikes
Talking about your career plans.

The Working Day

Here is a letter which might have been written by a young French boy to his pen-pal in England. His dad has a new job and they have moved house.

Tourlin
le 15 septembre 1992

Cher Gary,

C'est la première lettre que j'écris depuis la nouvelle maison. Nous avons déménagé lundi dernier. Ma nouvelle adresse est:

110, avenue des Peupliers
Tourlin
Yonne.

Papa a un nouvel emploi. Il travaille comme mécanicien dans une grande usine près d'ici. Il quitte la maison à sept heures et demie pour commencer son travail à huit heures. Il finit son travail à cinq heures et demie, et il rentre chez nous vers six heures. Il ne travaille pas le samedi.

Moi, je vais au collège Lafayette. C'est un très grand CES, qui a 1800 élèves. Les cours commencent à neuf heures moins le quart et finissent à quatre heures. La récréation est à dix heures et demie, et nous mangeons à midi et demi à la cantine. Je vais au collège en vélo, car ce n'est pas très loin d'ici. Mon copain, qui s'appelle Jean-Pierre, habite près de chez nous, et nous allons au collège ensemble.

The Working Day

> Il y a six cours par jour. Ma matière préférée est la géographie. Nous avons géo trois fois par semaine. Je déteste le lundi, car nous avons deux cours de maths — Je ne suis pas très fort en maths, tu sais...

This letter contains much of the type of information you will be expected to give in the Speaking and Writing tasks. You will need to talk or write about where members of your family work, what job you would like, your school, and if you plan to study or work after the exams.

Now listen to Marc being interviewed about his school, his timetable, and what he likes and dislikes.

To talk or write about these, you can use the following:

Where people (would like to) work

Now Mon père Mon frère Ma mère Ma soeur Je	travaille dans	une usine un café un bureau une banque un atelier un hôpital
Later Je voudrais travailler dans		

What people are (or would like to be)

		Male	Female
Mon père Mon frère	est	boulanger garagiste vendeur	
Ma mère Ma soeur			institutrice vendeuse
Je voudrais être		mécanicien coiffeur ·	mécanicienne coiffeuse

The Working Day

- Note *en chômage* = unemployed.
- Note also *retraité(e)* = retired.
- You will need to collect the vocabulary for typical jobs and workplaces, as well as those you need for your family and friends.

Your school's name

Mon	collège / lycée	s'appelle ...

Its location

Mon	collège / lycée	se trouve	à ... / près de ...
Il			

Its size

Il est	très grand / assez grand / tout petit

Number of pupils and teachers

Il y a	... élèves / ... étudiants / ... professeurs

School start and finish

Les cours	commencent / finissent	à ... heures

Break and lunch

La récréation / Le déjeuner	est à ... heures

Subjects

Je fais	des maths / des sciences / de l'anglais / de la musique / du français

Length of study

J'étudie / J'apprends	les maths / les sciences / l'anglais / la musique / le français	depuis ... ans

Liking or disliking

J'adore	le sport
J'aime bien	le français
Je n'aime pas	l'histoire
Je déteste	etc.

Favourite subject

| Ma matière préférée, c'est ... |

Your future study

Je vais	passer en première		pour faire du/de la/des ...	
Je veux J'espère	aller	au collège à l'université	pour étudier	le/la ... l'/les ...

Preparation

Make sure you know how to describe your school, talk about your timetable, etc. If you plan to study rather than work, check the words for colleges, etc.

Written Tasks You Might Be Set

1. Write a brief description of your school for your exchange school magazine.
2. Write to your (new) pen-friend, giving full details of your school day, subjects, etc.
3. Compile a C.V., filling in your personal details (see Chapter 1), and details of your school subjects and work.
4. Write a brief letter of application for a job in a hotel in France during the next holidays. (For letter outline, see Skills Guide, page 116.)

8 Health and Accidents

In this chapter, you will cover just the following:
Talking about what is wrong with someone
Talking about what people have injured
Requesting remedies
Arranging for treatment.

Something Wrong

Listen to the two model dialogues on the cassette. In the first, Julie is telling Martine what is wrong with her. In the second, Julie is discussing her illness with the doctor.

Here are some simple ways of talking about:

Illness

J'ai Il a Elle a	mal	à la tête à la gorge aux dents au ventre à la jambe au bras au coeur

Je suis Il est Elle est	malade enrhumé(e) constipé(e)
J'ai Il a Elle a	de la fièvre la grippe la diarrhée

Accidents

Je me suis Il s'est Elle s'est	blessé brûlé coupé cassé	la jambe la main le bras le pied le dos le genou

Remedies

Je voudrais Avez-vous	quelque chose des comprimés	pour	ma tête(?) ma gorge(?) mon dos(?) mon ventre(?)
Pourriez-vous me donner une ordonnance (a prescription) *?*			

Something Wrong

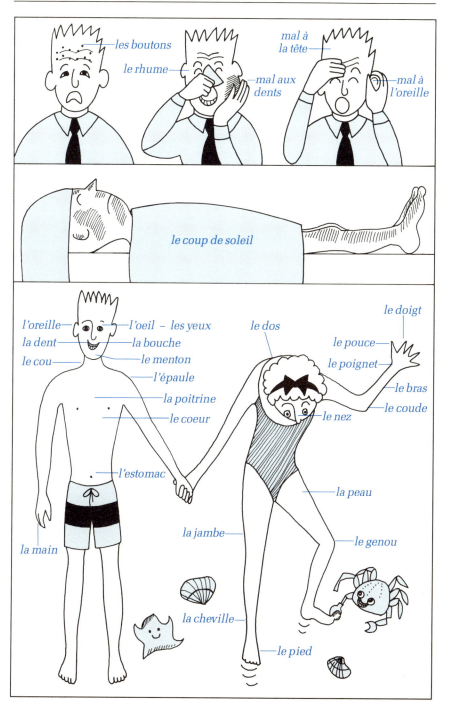

Something Wrong

You may also need to ask the following questions.

Requests

Est-ce que	je pourrais prendre rendez-vous?		
	vous pourriez appeler	un	médecin? docteur?
		une ambulance?	
	vous pourriez me donner un reçu? vous pourriez me préparer cette ordonnance?		

Rôle-plays

You may be asked to do a rôle-play at the chemist's or at the doctor's. You will not be expected to know every ailment! If you learn these basics and use your common sense to adapt them, you should cope with what is set.

Look at the following example of the type of rôle-play you may be set.

> You are staying at your pen-friend's and his/her parent has sent for the doctor because you aren't feeling well,
> - *1* – Say you've got a temperature and pains in your stomach.
> - *2* – Say you've been ill for two days.
> - *3* – Say you ate snails, and chicken and chips.
> - *4* – Ask how often you must take the tablets.

 Now listen to the same item on the tape.

Written Tasks

You may be asked to write an account of an accident. For this, you will need the past perfect of verbs such as:

tomber	*se blesser*	*aller à l'hôpital*
se casser	*appeler une ambulance*	*rester au lit*

- NB: *heurter* = crash into.
- Follow the normal patterns (see Structures Guide, page 117), keep to the French you know, and it will not be as difficult as it first seemed.

9 Travel, Customs, At the Garage

Although written tasks are not unknown, the productive elements of this topic are predominantly oral.

Travel

The Travel element may occur as a topic in its own right, but it will also figure in other topics such as: school and work, leisure, holidays, etc. You may be asked about how you get to school, or how you get home from the supermarket or disco (present tense). You may also be asked to describe the journey when you last went on holiday (past tense).

🖭 First, listen to the model interview, number 1 on the tape. Marianne is talking about how she gets to and from school.

You may be asked such questions as:

> *Tu viens au collège à pied?*
> *Comment est-ce que tu rentres à la maison?*
> *Pas en voiture?*
> *Qu'est-ce que tu fais pendant le trajet en autobus?*
> *Pourquoi est-ce que tu n'y vas pas à pied?*

For such questions, you will need the basic expressions:

Je prends	*l'autobus* *le train* *un taxi* *le métro*

Je vais	*à ...* *au ...* *à la ...* (+ place)	*en*	*autobus* *vélo* *voiture*
Je viens		*à*	*bicyclette* *pied*
Je rentre		*par le*	*train* *métro*

You may also be asked why? (*Pourquoi?*). If so, you will need:

(*Parce que*)	*ça va plus vite qu'en* ... *c'est moins cher qu'en* ...
(*Parce qu'*)	*il n'y a pas de (d')* ...

You may also be asked about how you spend the journey. (*Qu'est-ce que tu fais pendant le trajet?*) Your answers may include:

Je bavarde	*avec mes amis*
Je regarde	*par la fenêtre*
Je lis	*mon livre* *un magazine*
Je fais	*mes devoirs!*

If you are asked to talk or write about a holiday journey, you will need past tenses, particulary the past perfect (*passé composé*).

Listen to Martin being interviewed about his journey to Bordeaux, number 2 on the tape. Because he didn't travel on his own, he is answering in the plural form *nous*.

> *Alors, Martin, tu es allé à Bordeaux samedi dernier?*
> *Comment est-ce que tu y es allé?*
> *Le voyage était long?*
> *Vous êtes partis à quelle heure?*
> *Qu'est-ce que vous avez fait pendant le voyage?*
> *C'était comment, le voyage?*

To talk or write about journeys, you will need the following:

How you travelled

Nous <u>sommes allés</u> en *Nous <u>avons pris</u> le/la/l'*	*voiture* *car* *bateau* *avion* *aéroglisseur*

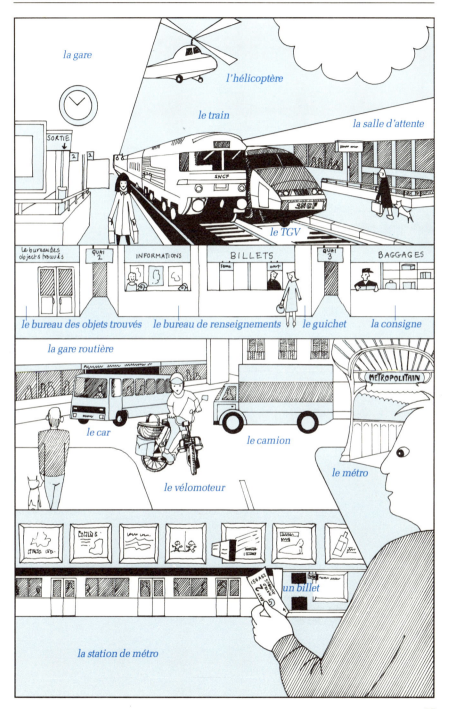

Travel

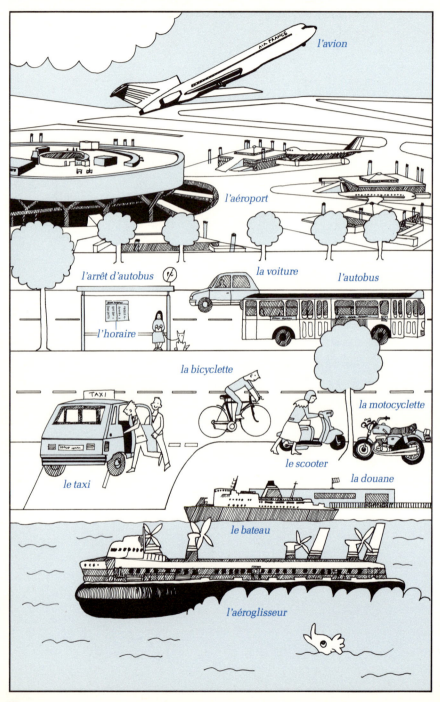

How long the journey took

Le voyage a duré	trois heures douze heures toute la journée

When you set off or arrived

Nous sommes	partis arrivés	à midi à trois heures à minuit

What you did on the journey

J'ai Nous avons	mangé des bonbons regardé un film regardé le paysage lu un magazine bu un coca écouté des cassettes joué aux cartes	
	pris le	petit déjeuner déjeuner dîner
	dormi	

What it was like

Le voyage était	long fatigant ennuyeux rapide intéressant

At the Station, etc.

There are many important rôle-plays involving travel.

Listen to the model dialogue at the station information office, number 1 on the tape. A tourist is enquiring about a train journey to Bordeaux. It demonstrates the sort of rôle you might be asked to play.

At the Station

You may need to:

Book or buy a ticket

Je voudrais	un aller simple un aller-retour	(en première/ seconde)	pour ...

Say when you want to travel

Je voudrais partir	ce matin cet après-midi demain la semaine prochaine

Say where you are going

Je veux aller	à (town) en (country) i.e. <u>name</u> of country

Ask when there is a bus, train, etc.

Il y a	un autobus un car un train un bateau une correspondance	à quelle heure?

Ask about the timetable

Le train L'avion	pour (place)	part arrive	à quelle heure?

Ask about changing

Il faut changer?	or	C'est un	train vol	direct?

Check which platform

C'est quel quai?

Book a seat

Je voudrais réserver une place, s'il vous plaît

Je voudrais une place	près de	la portière
		la fenêtre
	dans un compartiment non-fumeurs	

Customs

This is a small but important element in rôle-play. You may have to talk about yourself, your journey, or what you have with you.

You should be able to give most personal details on the basis of Chapter 1: Self and Family. You may be asked for your nationality or country of origin:

| Je suis | Anglais/Anglaise
Ecossais/Ecossaise
Gallois/Galloise
Irlandais/Irlandaise
Britannique | Je viens | d'Angleterre
d'Ecosse
du Pays de Galles
d'Irlande
de Grande-Bretagne |

Talk about your journey

| Je vais | à Nice |
| Je <u>vais passer</u> quinze jours | en France |

| Je viens | de Marseille | |
| J'<u>ai passé</u> | une semaine | à Marseille
en France |

Customs declaration

You may need to deal with a customs declaration:

| Est-ce que vous avez quelque chose à déclarer? |

| (Non) | Je n'ai rien à déclarer
J'ai seulement des cadeaux |

| (Oui!) | J'ai dix bouteilles de vin!
J'ai cinq cents cigarettes! |

At the Garage

Though you will not be expected to go into detail about the parts of the car, you will have to buy petrol/report simple faults.

First, buying petrol!

To ask for the quantity

Je voudrais	dix vingt	litres	d'essence (sans plomb)
	cent francs		de super

To have the tank filled

Faites le plein, s'il vous plaît

To ask for things to be checked

Voudriez-vous vérifier	la batterie l'huile l'eau les pneus	s'il vous plaît?

Now, to deal with a breakdown (simple!).

To say you have broken down

Je suis	(tombé(e))	en panne
Ma voiture est	(tombée)	

To ask for a mechanic

Pourriez-vous faire venir un mécanicien? Un mécanicien peut venir?

To say where you are stranded

Je suis	dans la rue principale sur la Route Nationale numéro ... en face de l'hypermarché près de Bonville entre Nice et Marseille sur le parking près ...

To say what the problem is

C'est	le moteur la batterie un pneu
Je n'ai pas d'essence	

Rôle-plays

🔲 Listen to the dialogue at the service station, number 2 on the tape.

You may have to give name, address or car number and spell them in French!

e.g. *Je m'appelle S-M-I-T-H*

You are *not* expected to know all the car parts or faults!

Read carefully these examples of the sort of rôle-play task you might be set on this unit.

> 1. You are at a French railway station, wanting to travel to Nantes.
> *1* – Ask for a second class, return ticket.
> *2* – Find out when there is a train.
> *3* – Check if you must change trains.

> 2. You are at the customs desk in Calais harbour. The official wants to know certain details.
> *1* – Give your nationality.
> *2* – Say you are going to your pen-friend's
> *3* – Tell the official how long you are going to stay.

🔲 Then listen to the sample rôle-plays, numbers 1 and 2 on the cassette.

10 Shopping, Banking and Post Office, Returns and Complaints

In this chapter you will cover:
Buying foods
Buying a present
Buying clothes
Cashing a traveller's cheque
Changing currency and cash
Buying stamps
Asking to phone
Returning goods.

Shopping for Food

Listen to the model dialogue, number 1 on the cassette. It shows you how to ask for certain quantities of food and revises the basic shopping phrases.

Here is a summary of how to buy food:

Je voudrais *Donnez-moi* *J'ai besoin* { *d'* *de*	*un paquet de* *une boîte de* *une plaque de* *un morceau de* *une bouteille de* *un kilo de* *une livre de* *200 grammes de* *deux tranches de* *cinq rondelles de* *un pot de*	*sucre* *coca* *beurre* *fromage* *vin rouge* *tomates* *pommes* *pâté* *jambon* *saucisson* *confiture*	*s'il vous plaît*

You may be asked: *C'est tout?*
If you have all you want, say: *Oui, merci.*
If you need more, say: *Non, je voudrais aussi . . .*
To ask what an item costs: *C'est combien, le jambon?*
To ask the total cost: *Ça fait combien?*
To pay the bill: *Voilà.*

Shopping for a Present

🎧 Listen to the model dialogue, number 2 on the cassette. Paul is trying to buy a present for his dad. It shows how to ask for advice and indicate what you want!

Here is a summary of the important phrases:

Je cherche un cadeau pour	*mon grand-père* *mon père* *mon frère* *ma mère* *ma soeur* *ma grand-mère*

Est-ce que vous pourriez	*m'aider?* *me donner un conseil?*

(Est-ce que) vous avez	*des briquets?* *des cendriers?* *des boîtes de bonbons?* *des bols?* *du parfum?*

Je voudrais *Je vais prendre*	*un briquet* *un cendrier* *une boîte* *un bol* *du parfum*	*comme ça*

- Don't forget to check the price and pay (see Shopping for Food, opposite).

Shopping for Clothes

🎧 Listen to the model dialogue, number 3 on the cassette. It shows you how to ask for clothing, deal with size, colour, fabric, trying on, agreeing or not agreeing to it. For this section, you will need to collect and learn items of clothing and colours and revise sizes.

Overleaf are the special phrases you will need.

Shopping for Clothes

What you want

Je cherche Je voudrais	un tee-shirt une jupe des { chaussures souliers des chaussettes	comme	celui celle	qui est	en vitrine
			ceux celles	qui sont	

Size: Clothes

Je prends la taille moyenne	
Je fais	la taille quarante-deux du quarante-deux

Size: Shoes

Je fais	trente-neuf de pointure du trente-neuf

Miscellaneous

C'est Il/elle est Ils/elles sont	en coton? en laine? en nylon? en cuir?

Vous	l' les	avez	en	bleu clair? jaune? noir? vert foncé?

Je peux	l' les	essayer,	s'il vous plaît?

C'est Il/elle est Ils/elles sont	trop	grand(e)(s) petit(e)(s) long(ue)(s) court(e)(s) étroit(e)(s)

Vous	l' les	avez	en (taille) quarante-quatre? en (pointure) trente-sept?

Bon! Ça me va bien		Je vais prendre ça

- N.B. Checking price and paying are included under Shopping for Food, page 64.

Banking

To talk about the various transactions, you can use the following:

Cashing a traveller's cheque

| Je voudrais | changer | ce chèque de voyage |
| | toucher | un chèque de dix livres sterling |

Changing currency

| Je voudrais changer | de l'argent anglais |
| | dix livres en francs |

Asking for notes or coins

Je voudrais	des billets de vingt francs(?)
Je peux avoir	des pièces d'un franc(?)
Avez-vous	de la monnaie (= small change)(?)

- Remember, you may be asked to sign, or produce your passport or identity card. You can respond with:

| Voilà, | monsieur / madame / mademoiselle |

At the Post Office

The following are useful:

Which stamps you need

C'est combien pour	une carte postale	pour l'Angleterre?
	une lettre	pour l'étranger
	un paquet	

How many stamps to buy

| Donnez-moi | un timbre | à quatre-vingts centimes |
| Je voudrais | quatre timbres | à un franc vingt |

Sending a telegram

| Je voudrais | envoyer un télégramme? |
| Est-ce qu'on peut | |

Telephoning – Miscellaneous

Où se trouve la cabine téléphonique?	Where is the phone box?
Est-ce que je peux téléphoner d'ici?	Can I phone from here?
Avez-vous l'annuaire?	Have you the phone book?
Je voudrais téléphoner en Angleterre.	I would like to phone England.
Voudriez-vous prendre un message?	Will you take a message?
Le trente-six, quarante-deux, quinze.	36 42 15.
Je vous dois combien?	How much do I owe you?

Returns and Complaints

To say you want to complain, you can use:

Je voudrais me plaindre.

Say what you bought, and when

J'ai acheté	ce pull cette jupe cette montre	ce matin hier samedi dernier

Say what is wrong with it

C'est Il/elle est	trop grand(e) trop étroit(e) = trop petit(e)
C'est Il/elle est	cassé(e)
Ça ne marche pas	

Say what you want

Vous pouvez l'échanger?	
Vous l'avez en plus	grand? petit?
Vous pouvez le/la réparer? Vous pouvez me rembourser?	

Proof of purchase

Voici le reçu. Je regrette. J'ai perdu le reçu.

Now listen to the model dialogue, number 4 on the cassette. Julien is complaining about a sweater he has bought.

Verbs: verb agreement

Structures Guide

Section 1 – Verbs

Verbs are the most important structure in any language. It is true that you can respond to questions with short answers such as *'Oui', 'En autobus', 'Dans le jardin', 'A huit heures',* etc. in a very natural and correct way. But if you want to convey a complete idea (whether speaking or writing), you must use a full sentence.

A verb is the key structure or 'backbone' in any sentence. It specifies:
a) what the activity is, and
b) whether the activity <u>has</u> happened already, <u>will</u> happen later, or is happening <u>now</u> or regularly.

In French, verbs change their form to show who or what is 'doing' them (called 'agreement') and when they are being done (called 'tense').

Verb agreement

There are eight possible agreements of a verb, each one linked to a personal 'pronoun'. The eight pronouns are:

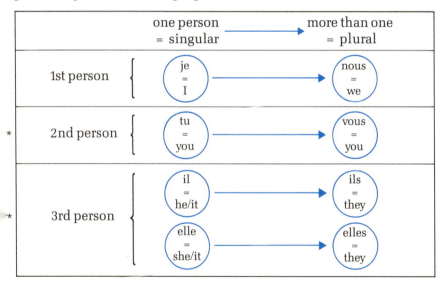

There is also a very useful pronoun, *on*, which can mean 'one' or 'you' or 'people' generally. This needs the same form of the verb as *il*.

*You. `tu` is the word you use to a friend, a relative, a child.
`vous` is the word you use to friends, relatives, children *PLUS* an adult stranger or strangers.

**He, she, they. Often, you will want to use a name or a relative instead of the pronoun.

Verb tenses

There are many tenses of verb which show the different 'time areas' of an activity. The most important tenses are:

The Present – Now or generally
The Future – Looking ahead
The Pasts – Looking back

Another useful tense is the Conditional, looking ahead to what might happen if . . .

Present tense

This is used to describe what <u>is happening</u> now or what <u>does happen</u> generally.

In English, the present may need one or two verb-words.

e.g. Paul <u>is eating</u> an apple.
<u>Does</u> Paul <u>eat</u> cheese?
Paul <u>eats</u> some toast at 8 a.m.

In French, the present is always a one verb-word tense.

e.g. *Paul <u>mange</u> une pomme.*
Est-ce que Paul <u>mange</u> du fromage?
Paul <u>mange</u> du pain grillé à huit heures.

Paul mange du pain grillé à huit heures

There are two kinds of verbs in French:
a) regular verbs which follow certain set patterns;
b) irregular verbs which have their own, individual forms.

Regular verb patterns

There are three regular set patterns which are known as:
  -*er* (like *por<u>ter</u>*)
  -*ir* (like *fin<u>ir</u>*)
  -*re* (like *ven<u>dre</u>*).
referring to the final two letters of the title form.

Verbs: present tense

The -*er* pattern (the easiest and largest group of verbs).
  To work out the eight verb agreements, you:
    take off the -*er*
    which leaves the stem,
    then add these letters:
  e.g. *porter* = to carry or wear
    port + -*er*

je port**e**	*nous* port**ons**
tu port**es**	*vous* port**ez**
il port**e**	*ils* port**ent**
elle port**e**	*elles* port**ent**

• The good news is that most of the endings don't sound! All six parts shaded sound the same – *port!*

The -*ir* pattern
  To work out the eight agreements, you:
    take off the -*ir*
    which leaves the stem,
    then add these letters:
  e.g. *finir* = to finish
    fin + -*ir*

je fin**is**	*nous* fin**issons**
tu fin**is**	*vous* fin**issez**
il fin**it**	*ils* fin**issent**
elle fin**it**	*elles* fin**issent**

• Although these endings do sound, the four parts shaded sound the same (*finee*). The *finissent* forms are pronounced *fin*ee**ss**.

The -*re* pattern
  To work out the eight forms, you:
    take off the -*re*
    which leaves the stem,
    then add these letters:
  e.g. *vendre* = to sell
    vend + -*re*

je vend**s**	*nous* vend**ons**
tu vend**s**	*vous* vend**ez**
il vend	*ils* vend**ent**
elle vend	*elles* vend**ent**

• Note that the shaded parts again sound similar.

Verses: present tense

The big four

Irregular verbs – the big four

These are the four verbs used most frequently. They are also the most irregular, so it is essential that you learn them.

1. être
- own meaning 'to be'
- also used to form past perfect tense of *some* verbs

* = 's' sound

2. avoir
- own meaning 'to have'
- also used to form past perfect tense of *most* verbs
- also used in special idioms

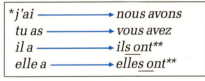

**j'ai* = two words, short for *je ai*.
** = 'z' sound

3. aller
- own meaning 'to go'
- also used to form the (easy) future tense

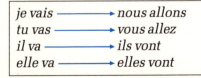

4. faire
- own meaning 'to do' or 'make'
- also used in special idioms

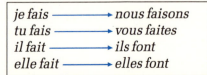

Irregular verbs – the rest

There are many verbs which vary from, or do not follow, one of the regular patterns.

Here are the TOP TWENTY.

acheter to buy (also *lever* to lift)

j'ach**è**te → nous achetons	we
tu ach**è**tes → vous achetez	you
il ach**è**te → ils ach**è**tent	they
elle ach**è**te → elles ach**è**tent	they

dire to say

| je dis → nous disons |
| tu dis → vous dites |
| il dit → ils disent |
| elle dit → elles disent |

appeler to call (also *jeter* to throw)

| j'appelle → nous appelons |
| tu appelles → vous apelez |
| il appelle → ils appellent |
| elle appelle → elles appellent |

dormir to sleep

| je dors → nous dormons |
| tu dors → vous dormez |
| il dort → ils dorment |
| elle dort → elles dorment |

boire to drink

| je bois → nous buvons |
| tu bois → vous buvez |
| il boit → ils boivent |
| elle boit → elles boivent |

écrire to write

| j'écris → nous écrivons |
| tu écris → vous écrivez |
| il écrit → ils écrivent |
| elle écrit → elles écrivent |

commencer to begin
(also *lancer* to throw)

| je commence → nous commençons |
| tu commences → vous commencez |
| il commence → ils commencent |
| elle commence → elles commencent |

lire to read

| je lis → nous lisons |
| tu lis → vous lisez |
| il lit → ils lisent |
| elle lit → elles lisent |

connaître to know (person/place)

| je connais → nous connaissons |
| tu connais → vous connaissez |
| il connait → ils connaissent |
| elle connait → elles connaissent |

manger to eat (also *nager* to swim)

| je mange → nous mangeons |
| tu manges → vous mangez |
| il mange → ils mangent |
| elle mange → elles mangent |

Verbs: present tense

mettre to put (on)

je mets	→ nous mettons
tu mets	→ vous mettez
il met	→ ils mettent
elle met	→ elles mettent

savoir to know (something)

je sais	→ nous savons
tu sais	→ vous savez
il sait	→ ils savent
elle sait	→ elles savent

ouvrir to open

j'ouvre	→ nous ouvrons
tu ouvres	→ vous ouvrez
il ouvre	→ ils ouvrent
elle ouvre	→ elles ouvrent

sortir to go out

je sors	→ nous sortons
tu sors	→ vous sortez
il sort	→ ils sortent
elle sort	→ elles sortent

partir to set off

je pars	→ nous partons
tu pars	→ vous partez
il part	→ ils partent
elle part	→ elles partent

tenir to hold

je tiens	→ nous tenons
tu tiens	→ vous tenez
il tient	→ ils tiennent
elle tient	→ elles tiennent

préférer to prefer
(also *espérer* to hope)

je préfère	→ nous préférons
tu préfères	→ vous préférez
il préfère	→ ils préfèrent
elle préfère	→ elles préfèrent

venir to come

je viens	→ nous venons
tu viens	→ vous venez
il vient	→ ils viennent
elle vient	→ elles viennent

prendre to take

je prends	→ nous prenons
tu prends	→ vous prenez
il prend	→ ils prennent
elle prend	→ elles prennent

voir to see

je vois	→ nous voyons
tu vois	→ vous voyez
il voit	→ ils voient
elle voit	→ elles voient

These twenty verbs are here for your reference. Don't panic about trying to learn <u>all</u> of <u>all</u> of them!

Think which parts you are most likely to need:

Verbs: present tense

> The *je* part to talk or write about yourself.
>
> The *il* or *elle* part to talk or write about your friend or a relative – this is very often the same as, or similar to, the *je* part.
>
> The *nous* part for leisure and holidays – remember the *-ons* ending!
>
> If you are talking about your brothers or sisters, the *ils* or *elles* part often sounds like the *il* or *elle* part; if you are writing, remember the *-ent* ending.

Verbs – Extra

In addition to these basic regular and irregular verbs, there are several important verbs (some regular, some irregular in themselves) which need an additional, special structure. These are reflexive verbs, and verbs which need a second verb:

Reflexive verbs

These verbs describe things 'you do to yourself', and are used most when talking or writing about your routine. They can be recognised by the *se* in the dictionary or vocabulary list, and by the *me* when referring to yourself.

A typical reflexive verb is *se laver* 'to get washed'. The eight forms in the present tense are given below left:

je **me** lave	nous **nous** lavons	je **me** lève	nous **nous** levons
tu **te** laves	vous **vous** lavez	tu **te** lèves	vous **vous** levez
il **se** lave	ils **se** lavent	il **se** lève	ils **se** lèvent
elle **se** lave	elles **se** lavent	elle **se** lève	elles **se** lèvent

Se laver is a regular, reflexive verb. It must not be confused with the similar, but irregular, reflexive verb *se lever* 'to get up', given above right.

- The *me, te, se, nous, vous* will be needed with such reflexive verbs in *all* tenses.

Verbs needing a second verb

These very useful verbs may themselves be regular or irregular, but because they convey only part of the meaning, they need a second verb to complete the meaning.

The verbs *vouloir, pouvoir* and *devoir* are special – but useful!

Verbs: present tense

They can be used in a variety of situations. They are particularly useful for talking about what you can do in a town or resort, and what you are allowed or have to do, etc.

They form a special group, being partly irregular and needing a special pattern. This involves using a second verb to complete the meaning. The second verb is always the same – the infinitive or title form of the verb.

vouloir to want	
je veux ⟶	nous voulons
tu veux ⟶	vous voulez
il, elle } veut ⟶	ils, elles } veulent

pouvoir	to be able / to be allowed
je peux ⟶	nous pouvons
tu peux ⟶	vous pouvez
il, elle } peut ⟶	ils, elles } peuvent

Another form of *vouloir* can be used in the same way. This is the conditional tense, meaning 'would like'.

je voudrais ⟶	nous voudrions
tu voudrais ⟶	vous voudriez
il, elle } voudrait ⟶	ils, elles } voudraient

devoir to have to	
je dois ⟶	nous devons
tu dois ⟶	vous devez
il, elle } doit ⟶	ils, elles } doivent

● Useful instead of *devoir* is *il faut* meaning 'it's necessary'.

Some examples:
Samedi soir, je <u>peux sortir</u> avec mes amis.
On <u>peut faire</u> une promenade dans le parc.
Je <u>dois faire</u> des achats avant de dîner.
Il <u>faut aller</u> au collège tous les jours!

On peut faire une promenade dans le parc

Verbs: past tenses

Past tenses

There is no such thing as <u>the</u> past tense in French. There are several past tenses which enable us to talk and write about things that happened at various times in the past.

The past perfect *(passé composé)*

This is the most important past tense. It is used to describe events which happened or have happened. In English, we may use one or two words to describe the activity:

I <u>ate</u>/I <u>have eaten</u>   or   He <u>arrived</u>/He <u>has arrived</u>.

In French, the most important thing to remember about the past perfect is that <u>it always needs two verb words.</u> There are three groups of verbs in the past perfect: *avoir* verbs, *être* verbs, and reflexive verbs.

Avoir verbs

These form by far the largest group.

<u>The first verb-word</u> indicates that the activity is past and refers to the person involved. This first verb-word must be part of the present tense of *avoir* 'to have'.

So, to say:

    I ,   you need *j'<u>ai</u>**
    he ,   you need *il <u>a</u>*
    she ,   you need *elle <u>a</u>*

For the other possibilities, see the present tense of *avoir,* page 72.

**J'<u>ai</u>* is really two words, *je + ai*, put together to make them easier to say.
Many candidates confuse this with *je* = I.

<u>The second verb-word</u> indicates what activity happened and is called the past participle. Normally, this is formed from the <u>title form</u> (= infinitive) of the verb in question. If the verb is regular and follows the set pattern, the past participle is easy to make up.

If the infinitive ends in *-er*, the past participle ends in *é* ('e' acute).

    e.g. *regarder* ⟶ *regardé**
         porter ⟶ *porté**

*Note that this *é* ending is pronounced 'ay' and must not be confused with the silent *e* on the present tense – *je regarde, je porte.*

If the infinitive ends in *-ir*, the past participle ends in *i*.

    e.g. *finir* ⟶ *fini*
         choisir ⟶ *choisi*

If the infinitive ends in *-re,* the past participle ends in *u*.

    e.g. *vendre* ⟶ *vendu*
         attendre ⟶ *attendu*

Verbs: past tenses

Unfortunately, there are several verbs which are irregular and do <u>not</u> form the past participle according to the set pattern. Some of the more important irregular past participles are listed at the end of this section on page 84.

So, to make the past perfect of this group of verbs you need:

First verb-word		Second verb-word
= part of *avoir*		= past participle of verb
= to have.	+	showing the activity.
This must agree with the person doing the activity.		This is the same for any person doing the activity.

e.g. *J'<u>ai</u> + <u>choisi</u> une glace aux fraises.*
Mon frère <u>a</u> + <u>choisi</u> une portion de frites.

<u>Etre</u> ver<u>b</u>s

The verbs which form the past perfect with parts of *être* form a special group of thirteen, mostly concerned with movement. In this group, the <u>first verb-word</u>, which refers to the person involved in the activity, is part of the present tense of *être* 'to be' (instead of *avoir* 'to have'). However, it still conveys the general meaning of 'have', and you must not fall into the trap of thinking that it is connected with the English 'he is going', which is a present tense.

aller → *allé* to go	and	*venir* → *venu* to come
entrer → *entré* to go in	and	*sortir* → *sorti* to go out
monter → *monté* to climb up	and	*descendre* → *descendu* to go down
arriver → *arrivé* to arrive	and	*partir* → *parti* to set off
tomber → *tombé* to fall	and	*rester* → *resté* to stay
naître → *né* to be born	and	*mourir* → *mort* to die
rentrer → *rentré* to come back (home)	or	*retourner* → *retourné* to return

Verbs: past tenses

With these verbs, to say:
    I,   you need *je suis*
    he,   you need *il est*
    she, you need *elle est*
    etc.
- For the rest, see page 77.

The past participles of these verbs are formed on the same basis as the *avoir* group. As can be seen from the above chart, some are regular and some are irregular. However, these past participles, unlike those in the previous group, do not always stay the same.

To be accurate, you should change the ending of the past participle to match the person who you are referring to. Thus:

If you are referring to a female or feminine noun – add an *e*.

So, a boy writing about himself writes:
    Je suis allé
But a girl writing about herself should write:
    Je suis allée
Anyone writing about a male should put:
    Philippe est allé
Anyone writing about a female should put:
    Danielle est allée

Also:

If you are referring to more than one male or masculine noun – add an *s*.

---

    e.g. *Philippe et André sont allés à la piscine.*

If you are referring to more than one female or feminine noun – add *es*.

---

    e.g. *Marie et Danielle sont allées en ville.*

But:

If you are referring to more than one person, male *and* female – add an *s*.

---

    e.g. *Philippe et Danielle sont allés au cinéma.*
        Mes parents sont allés au bord de la mer.

Verbs: past tenses

So, to make the past perfect of this group of verbs, you need:

| First verb-word = part of *être* = to be. This must 'agree' with the person doing the activity. | + | Second verb-word = past participle of verb showing the activity. This will have *e* added when referring to female + *s* for more than one. |

Reflexive verbs

The group of verbs called 'reflexives', which often describe things 'you do to yourself' (see page 75), also needs to use part of the verb *être* as the first verb word.

You can easily recognise these reflexive verbs because they always have *me, te, se* or an extra *nous* or *vous* to refer back to the person(s) speaking.

With these verbs, to say:

    I,   you need *je me suis*
    he, you need *il s'est*
    she, you need *elle s'est*
    we, you need *nous nous sommes.*

The past participles of these verbs are formed on the same basis as the first group, some regular and some irregular; but to be accurate, you should add *e/s/es* to the end of these past participles when referring back to females or plurals, as in the previous group.

Thus: *Je me suis réveillé à sept heures.* (boy writing)
but: *Je me suis réveillée à . . .* (girl writing)
And: *Il s'est vite habillé.*
but: *Elle s'est habillée dans la salle de bains.*
Also: *Les enfants se sont vite habillés.*

Les enfants se sont vite habillés

How to work out which group

First tackle the second verb word (past participle). If you can't remember it, look it up in your verb list or dictionary.

If it is not listed as irregular, then assume it is regular and apply the

-er é
-ir i } rule (see page 77);
-re u

then decide on *avoir* or *être*. How?

Work backwards through the last three sections:

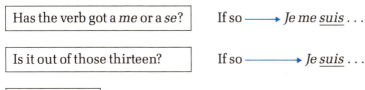

| Is it neither? | Then it must be *J'ai* . . . Most verbs are! |

Worried about the *e* and *s* endings?

Don't be! When you are talking in French, you can't hear these extra *e* and *s* endings (except in *morte/mortes*!). Because of this, many French people do not write them properly either, and you can communicate your ideas perfectly well without them.

- Learn the 'je' part of each verb first.
- Learn how to convert:

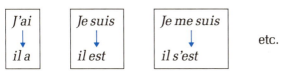

etc.

- Check that you have two verb-words; it is a good idea to check this by underlining them both, as you can see here:

J'ai acheté un disque.
Elle est allée en ville.
Il a mangé une glace.
Je me suis levé à neuf heures.

Preparation

If you have not already done so, start your own collection (three groups – three lists) of verbs in the past perfect as you use them or have them marked.

e.g. *manger*, eat   *J'ai mangé*
     se lever, get up   *Je me suis levé*

Verbs: past tenses

The past imperfect (*imparfait*)

This is a very simple past tense used to describe situations which <u>did exist</u>, and events which <u>were happening</u> or <u>used to happen</u> over a period of time in the past.

In English, we often use two or more words to describe the situation or activity:

      He <u>was playing</u>/He <u>used to play</u>   or   We <u>had</u>/We <u>used to have</u>.

In French, the past imperfect is a one verb-word tense, and most verbs follow the same pattern.

Etre 'to be' is the verb used most in the past imperfect. It is irregular and has to be learnt:

j'étais	nous étions
tu étais	vous étiez
il était	ils étaient
elle était	elles étaient

To make the past imperfect of almost all other verbs, you simply work out the *nous* part of the present tense (remember to check the 'big four' and the 'irregulars'), remove the *-ons* ending and then add a special set of imperfect endings. So, to form the past imperfect of *prendre*:

present tense (*nous* part) = *prenons*
remove *-ons* = *pren*
add imperfect endings:

je + ais   il   nous + <u>ions</u>   ils
tu + ais   elle } + ait   vous + <u>iez</u>   elles } + aient

Irregular
avoir 'to have' becomes:

j'av**ais**	nous av**ions**
tu av**ais**	vous av**iez**
il av**ait**	ils av**aient**
elle av**ait**	elles av**aient**

-er
jouer 'to play' becomes:

je jou**ais**	nous jou**ions**
tu jou**ais**	vous jou**iez**
il jou**ait**	ils jou**aient**
elle jou**ait**	elles jou**aient**

-re
vendre 'to sell' becomes:

je vend**ais**	nous vend**ions**
tu vend**ais**	vous vend**iez**
il vend**ait**	ils vend**aient**
elle vend**ait**	elles vend**aient**

-ir
finir 'to finish' becomes:

je finiss**ais**	nous finiss**ions**
tu finiss**ais**	vous finiss**iez**
il finiss**ait**	ils finiss**aient**
elle finiss**ait**	elles finiss**aient**

Verbs: past tenses

The past imperfect is particularly useful for describing what your holiday hotel or camp-site was like, using such phrases as:

C'était...
Il se trouvait...
Il y avait... (There was...)

or what it was like in the French home where you may have stayed:

C'était formidable!
L'appartement se trouvait...
Il y avait deux garçons...
Le père était professeur...

or what the weather was like:

Il faisait froid
Il faisait du soleil   } *Il* form only!
Il pleuvait

Il faisait du soleil

The past pluperfect *(plus-que-parfait)*

This is a special past tense which you might need in order to talk or write about things which <u>had already happened</u> before the events you are describing in the past perfect tense.

So, you can think of it as a 'double past' tense:
   a) because it describes two steps back in time,
and b) because of the way it is constructed.

The past pluperfect is another tense which needs two verb-words in French. It is similar to the past perfect in that:
1. it uses the same past participle to show the activity;
2. it uses part of *avoir* or *être* to link to the person doing the activity;
3. it divides verbs into the same three groups
   a) *avoir* verbs
   b) *être* verbs
   c) reflexive verbs

Where it is different from the past perfect lies in what we do with the *avoir* or *être* which forms the first verb-word. Whereas in the past perfect, we use the present of *avoir* or *être*:
> e.g. *J'**ai** regardé la télé.*
> *Nous **sommes** arrivés en retard.*
> *Nous nous **sommes** habillés très vite.*

in the past pluperfect, we use the past imperfect of *avoir* or *être*:
> e.g. *J'**avais** regardé la télé.*
> *Nous **étions** arrivés en retard.*
> *Nous nous **étions** habillés très vite.*

As you can see, the past pluperfect has a past of *avoir* or *être* for the first verb-word, and a past participle for the second verb-word.

Irregular past participles

For use as second verb word in past perfect and past pluperfect.

infinitive	(je form/ past perfect)	past participle	infinitive	(je form/ past perfect)	past participle
avoir	j'ai	eu	mourir	il est	mort
être	j'ai	été	naître	je suis	né
			ouvrir	j'ai	ouvert
boire	j'ai	bu	pouvoir	j'ai	pu
devoir	j'ai	dû	prendre	j'ai	pris
dire	j'ai	dit	rire	j'ai	ri
écrire	j'ai	écrit	tenir	j'ai	tenu
faire	j'ai	fait	venir	je suis	venu
lire	j'ai	lu	voir	j'ai	vu
mettre	j'ai	mis	vouloir	j'ai	voulu

Future tenses

There are two forms of the future tense, both of which can be used to describe activities which will be happening at some future time.

The future with 'aller' (*futur composé*)

The easier form is called the 'future with *aller*' (*futur composé*). It is used very frequently in conversational French and is recommended as the preferable tense if you find verbs difficult to learn.

The future with *aller* is made up of two verb-words and says what you are 'going to do'. There is just one pattern which is used for all activities:

Verbs: future tenses

First verb-word = part of *aller* = to go	+	Second verb-word = title or infinitive form of verb showing the activity

So, if you want to talk about what people are going to drink, you will need:

    for I,   *je vais*   + *boire un coca*
    for we,   *nous allons*   + *boire du thé*

If you want to talk about when people are going to arrive, you will need:

    for she,   *elle va*   + *arriver à midi*
    for they,   *ils vont*   + *arriver à une heure*

Do be careful if you need to say where people are going to go. You will need *aller* twice:

    for I,   *je vais*   + *aller à la piscine*
    for we,   *nous allons*   + *aller à la discothèque*

The simple future (*futur simple*)

The official form is called the 'simple future' (*futur simple*). It is more formal and is used frequently in written French. It is important that you can at least recognise this form, even if you choose not to use it.

The simple future is made up of just one verb-word and says what you 'will do'. Most verbs follow a regular pattern, but there are some irregular forms which you have to learn.

Regular

To form the simple future, you start with the title or infinitive form, then add a set of special endings.

So for an *-er* verb such as *porter*:	An *-ir* verb works in the same way; so for *finir*:
*je porter***ai** ⟶ *nous porter***ons** *tu porter***as** ⟶ *vous porter***ez** *il porter***a** ⟶ *ils porter***ont** *elle porter***a** ⟶ *elles porter***ont**	*je finir***ai** ⟶ *nous finir***ons** *tu finir***as** ⟶ *vous finir***ez** *il finir***a** ⟶ *ils finir***ont** *elle finir***a** ⟶ *elles finir***ont**

For an *-re* verb, there is a slight change. You start with the title form (infinitive), but take the *-e* off before adding the special endings.	So for *vendre*: *je vendr***ai** ⟶ *nous vendr***ons** *tu vendr***as** ⟶ *vous vendr***ez** *il vendr***a** ⟶ *ils vendr***ont** *elle vendr***a** ⟶ *elles vendr***ont**

Verbs: future tenses

- In the future tense, <u>all</u> the endings sound; *tu* and *il/elle* sound the same, and *nous* and *ils/elles* sound the same, as do *je* and *vous*.
- In the case of *-er* verbs, the *er* is unstressed and the endings stressed.

  e.g. *je port-e-ray*, etc.

Irregular

There are nearly a dozen important verbs which have their own individual form in the future. They use the same endings as the regular future, but have an irregular stem:

verb	*je* part	verb	*je* part
aller	*j'irai*	*savoir*	*je saurai*
avoir	*j'aurai*	*tenir*	*je tiendrai*
devoir	*je devrai*	*venir*	*je viendrai*
être	*je serai*	*voir*	*je verrai*
faire	*je ferai*	*vouloir*	*je voudrai*
pouvoir	*je pourrai*		

So, to write about what people will drink:

Je <u>boirai</u> un coca.

Nous <u>boirons</u> du thé.

To write about when people will arrive:

Elle <u>arrivera</u> à midi.

Ils <u>arriveront</u> à une heure.

To write about where people will go:

J'<u>irai</u> à la piscine.

Nous <u>irons</u> à la discothèque.

J'irai à la piscine

Summary of tenses

Past	Present (Regularly)	Future
Qu'est-ce que tu as fait…?	Qu'est-ce que tu fais… d'habitude?	Qu'est-ce que tu vas faire…?
…ce matin?…hier soir?	…le matin?…le soir?	…demain matin?…ce soir?
Je me suis levé(e) a…	Je me lève à…heures	Je vais me lever à…
J'ai préparé mon…	Je prépare mon petit déjeuner	Je vais préparer mon…
J'ai mangé…	Je prends mon petit déjeuner dans la cuisine	Je vais manger…
J'ai bu…	Je bois une tasse de café	Je vais boire…
J'ai lavé la vaisselle	Je lave la vaisselle	Je vais laver la vaisselle
Je suis allé(e) au collège…	Je vais au collège à …heures	Je vais aller au collège…
J'ai fait…	Je fais mes devoirs/mon lit	Je vais faire…
Je suis sorti(e) avec…	Je sors avec mon ami(e)	Je vais sortir avec…
J'ai écouté…	J'écoute la radio/mes disques	Je vais écouter…
J'ai regardé…	Je regarde la télé	Je vais regarder…
J'ai lu…	Je lis le journal/un livre	Je vais lire…
Je me suis couché(e) à…	Je me couche à …heures	Je vais me coucher à…
…samedi/dimanche/dernier? etc.	…le week-end/…pendant les vacances?	…samedi/dimanche prochain?
Je suis allé(e) en ville/à…	Je vais en ville/à…	Je vais aller en ville/à…
J'ai travaillé dans…	Je travaille dans…	Je vais travailler dans…
J'ai aidé ma mère…	J'aide ma mère/mon père dans…	Je vais aider ma mère…
J'ai joué au…/du…	Je joue au tennis/du piano	Je vais jouer au…/du…
J'ai visité…	Je visite…	Je vais visiter…
J'ai rencontré…	Je rencontre mes ami(e)s	Je vais rencontrer…
J'ai acheté…	J'achète…	Je vais acheter…

Genders: articles, adjectives

Section 2 – Genders

In English, gender plays a relatively minor rôle in the language. Most inanimate objects (i.e. 'things') are gender-less and regarded as 'it'.

In French, all nouns, whether they refer to people or things, have a gender and are regarded as masculine or feminine. With people, males are always masculine nouns, and females are usually feminine nouns; with things, there is no such obvious dividing line and genders have to be learnt, either by usage or by effort!

Using gender correctly will boost your grade in GCSE French. Once you know the correct gender of a noun, you will need to make sure that all words relating to that noun are adapted to agree with it. This applies to articles, e.g. *le*, *un*, *du*, etc., and other starting words, i.e. *ce*, *mon*, *son*, etc., as well as adjectives for colour, size, etc.

Articles

This chart shows you which 'starter' to pick for each gender and the plural:

Meaning	Before masculine noun	Before feminine noun	Before vowel (masculine)	Before vowel (feminine)	Before plural noun
a	un	une	un	une	(does not exist)
the	le	la	l'	l'	les
some	du	de la	de l'	de l'	des
this	ce	cette	cet	cette	ces
my	mon	ma	mon	mon	mes
your (if *tu* = you)	ton	ta	ton	ton	tes
his/her	son	sa	son	son	ses
our	notre	notre	notre	notre	nos
your (if *vous* = you)	votre	votre	votre	votre	vos
their	leur	leur	leur	leur	leurs

Adjectives

In French, whenever you use an adjective, you must make it 'agree' with (i.e. choose the right ending for) the gender of the noun you are referring to. This chart shows you how to make some of the most important adjectives 'agree'.

Genders: comparing with adjectives

Meaning	Masculine	Feminine	Before vowel (masculine)	Before vowel (feminine)	Plural Masculine	Plural Feminine
red	*rouge*	*rouge*	–	–	*rouges*	*rouges*
yellow	*jaune*	*jaune*	–	–	*jaunes*	*jaunes*
blue	*bleu*	*bleue*	–	–	*bleus*	*bleues*
black	*noir*	*noire*	–	–	*noirs*	*noires*
white	*blanc*	*blanche*	–	–	*blancs*	*blanches*
brown	*brun*	*brune*	–	–	*bruns*	*brunes*
grey	*gris*	*grise*	–	–	*gris*	*grises*
green	*vert*	*verte*	–	–	*verts*	*vertes*
large	*grand*	*grande*	*grand*	*grande*	*grands*	*grandes*
small	*petit*	*petite*	*petit*	*petite*	*petits*	*petites*
dear	*cher*	*chère*	*cher*	*chère*	*chers*	*chères*
beautiful	*beau*	*belle*	*bel*	*belle*	*beaux*	*belles*
new	*nouveau*	*nouvelle*	*nouvel*	*nouvelle*	*nouveaux*	*nouvelles*
old	*vieux*	*vieille*	*vieil*	*vieille*	*vieux*	*vieilles*

Note that if you use a colour with *clair* (light) or *foncé* (dark) attached, both words have no extra letters.
Thus: *Il porte des chaussures vertes.*
but: *Il porte des chaussures vert foncé.*

These agreements will apply whether you can use the adjective with the noun (common adjectives before the noun, colours and others after it), i.e. attributively; or later in the sentence, i.e. predicatively.
Thus, with the noun (attributively):
    Il porte un pantalon gris
    Nous avons une petite voiture.
Or, later in the sentence (predicatively):
    Son pantalon est gris
    Notre voiture est petite.

Comparing with adjectives

If you need to compare size, age, value, etc., by saying that one noun is bigger, older, more expensive, etc., than another, you must still make the adjective agree. In French, you usually compare by adding the word *plus* (= 'more').
  e.g. *La nouvelle maison est plus grande que l'appartement.*
      Les poires sont plus chères que les pommes.
      Ma soeur est plus âgée que mon frère.

Genders: singular and plural

- To express 'better', you use a special comparative adjective, *meilleur,* which must also 'agree'.

  e.g. *Les chats sont meilleurs que les chiens.*

Les chats sont meilleurs que les chiens

Comparing 'less than'

If you want to say that one noun is less tall, less expensive, etc., you add the word *moins* (= 'less') before the adjective. You must still make the adjective agree.

e.g. *Ma soeur est moins grande que mon frère.*
Cette jupe est moins chère que celle-là.

Singular and plural – how to adjust

We spend the vast majority of the time writing or talking about one person or one thing. However, if we need to write or talk about two or more brothers, pets, books, loaves, etc., we must use the plural form of the noun.

In French, most nouns are made plural by adding an *s*.

e.g. *un frère   trois frères   une pomme   six pommes*

But a few important nouns need an *x* instead. These nouns usually end in *-eau*.

e.g. *un gâteau   deux gâteaux   un oiseau   cinq oiseaux*

If you start your sentence with a plural noun, do not forget that your verb will also need to agree. Unlike the other words, this will not need an *s*. You will need to check the 'they' part of your verb and add the appropriate ending.

e.g. *J'ai un oiseau vert.*
J'ai deux oiseaux verts.

Ma soeur est jolie.
Mes soeurs sont jolies.

Mon amie française habite à Quimper.
Mes amies françaises habitent à Quimper.

- If you make the noun plural, you must make all the words which refer to it agree with the plural.

Section 3 – Prepositions

Prepositions are words which show the position or relationship of one word to another. French prepositions divide into three groups: simple prepositions; *de* prepositions; *à* prepositions.

Simple prepositions

These are single words and can simply be placed between the words in question – as in English. Some common examples are:

sur	on	*avec*	with
dans	in	*sans*	without
devant	in front of	*chez*	at home/shop of
derrière	behind	*par*	through
sous	under	*pour*	for
entre	between	*pendant*	during
parmi	amongst	*depuis*	since
après	after	*contre*	against
avant	before	*vers*	towards

e.g. *J'ai trouvé ma clef <u>sous</u> la chaise.*
Le chat s'est endormi <u>sur</u> mon lit.

'de' prepositions

Several important prepositions consist of one or two words plus *de*. Some common examples of the *de* prepositions are:

près de	near to	*le long de*	along
en face de	opposite to	*au bout de*	at the end of
à côté de	next to	*à cause de*	because of
au-dessus de	above	*autour de*	around
au-dessous de	beneath	*loin de*	far from

Whenever you use *de* with a noun, you must pay attention to the article in front of the noun. If *de* is needed in front of *le,* you must change the two words to *du.* If *de* is needed in front of *les,* you must change the two words to *des.*
- *de* + *le* = *du*
- *de* + *les* = *des*

Thus: | *Ma maison* | . . . | *près de* | + | *le collège* |

becomes: *Ma maison se trouve près <u>du</u> collège.*

Prepositions: 'à', 'depuis'

And: | Le parking | . . . | en face de | + | les magasins |

becomes: *Le parking se trouve en face des magasins.*

'à' prepositions

A few prepositions consist of more than one word and end in *à*. Some useful *à* prepositions are:

jusqu'à until   *grâce à* thanks to   *quant à* as for

As with the *de* prepositions, if these are used before a masculine or plural noun, you must use the special forms.

So: *Vous allez jusqu'à la boulangerie.*
But: *Nous allons rester jusqu'au premier juillet.*

'Depuis'

Depuis is a preposition which can be used in a special way. It has two meanings, 'since' (an event) and 'for a length of time' (looking back).

As 'since', it is quite straightforward, used in phrases such as:
   depuis ton arrivée   since your arrival
   depuis le déjeuner   since lunch

When you use *depuis* to mean 'for a length of time', you have to pay attention to the verb tense you use. In English, if we talk or write about something which has been going on for a period of time, and is still happening, we treat the continuous action as a past tense. In French, we must concentrate on the fact that the activity is still going on, and use the present tense.

   e.g. *J'apprends l'italien depuis trois ans.*
       I have been learning Italian for three years.

J'apprends l'italien depuis trois ans

Ma mère travaille dans ce bureau depuis cinq ans.
My mother has been working in this office for five years.

Section 4 – How to Make Questions

There are three ways to make questions in French. A fourth involves all three with question words.

1. The first, most popular way to make a question is to use a simple statement, and turn it into a question by adding a question mark, or using the correct intonation.

   e.g. *Il y a deux chambres.* There are two bedrooms.
   Il y a deux chambres? Are there two bedrooms?

   Elle est partie à six heures. She left at six.
   Elle est partie à six heures? Did she leave at six?

This technique is most useful in conversation.

2. The second, very easy way of making a question is to use the simple statement, but to turn it into a question by putting *Est-ce que . . .* before the statement.

   Est-ce qu'il y a deux chambres?
   Est-ce que maman est partie à six heures?

This technique is equally useful in spoken and written French, and is 'correct' in both.

3. The third way of making a question is more technical. You start with the statement and then reverse the subject (doer) and the verb. If the resulting word sequence is difficult to say, you may need to put in an extra *-t-*.

   Y a-t-il deux chambres?
   Est-elle partie à six heures?

This technique is best reserved for written work.

4. If you want to make a question using one of the question words, you can also do it in three ways.

   1 – First, using the statement:
   Il y a <u>combien</u> de chambres?
   Elle est partie <u>à quelle heure?</u>

   2 – Second, using *est-ce que*:
   <u>Combien</u> de chambres est-ce qu'il y a?
   <u>A quelle heure</u> est-ce qu'elle est partie?

   3 – Third, by reversing the statement:
   <u>Combien</u> de chambres y a-t-il?
   <u>A quelle heure</u> est-elle partie?

   • See Appendix 1, page 119, for a list of question words.

Negatives

Section 5 — How to Make Negatives

If you want to make a negative statement in French (i.e. say you 'don't like, aren't going, haven't finished', etc.), you must use *ne ... pas*. This is added to the basic statement by putting *ne* before the verb and *pas* after the verb.

So: *Il aime les maths.*
becomes: *Il n'aime pas les maths.*
And: *Nous avons de l'argent.*
becomes: *Nous n'avons pas d'argent.*

In the future and the past imperfect, *ne ... pas* is added in the same way.

Thus (future): *Elle ira en France.*
becomes: *Elle n'ira pas en France.*
And (past imperfect): *Il y avait beaucoup de monde.*
becomes: *Il n'y avait pas beaucoup de monde.*

If you are using a structure which has two verb-words (i.e. the past perfect, the 'future with *aller*', can, must, want), you must put *ne* and *pas* round the first, active verb-word.

So (past perfect): | *Il a joué au football*
 | *Il n'a pas joué au football.*

And (future with *aller*): | *Nous allons regarder la télévision*
 | *Nous n'allons pas regarder la télévision.*

Nous n'allons pas regarder la télévision

And (can, must, want): | *Je veux faire mes devoirs*
 | *Je ne veux pas faire mes devoirs.*

You will have noticed that after *ne ... pas*, words such as *du*, *de la*, *des*, change to plain *de*.

Using other negatives

There are several other negatives similar to *ne ... pas.* The two most important are:

    ne ... rien nothing   *ne ... jamais* never.

Both follow exactly the same pattern as *ne ... pas,* being added to the normal sentence round the verb-word or first verb-word.

  e.g. *Je ne vois rien.* I (can) see nothing.

    Elle n'est jamais allée en France. She has never been to France.

Je ne vois rien

Another useful negative is *ne ... personne,* meaning 'no one'. It is similar to *ne ... rien* and *ne ... jamais.*

So: *Je ne connais personne.*

But: *Je n'ai vu personne.*

Notice that *personne* goes <u>after</u> the past participle.

- If you want to say 'nothing' as a one-word answer, you simply use *rien.*

  e.g. *Qu'est-ce que tu as vu? – Rien!*

- Similarly, if you need 'never' as a one-word answer, use *jamais* on its own.

  e.g. *Tu as déjà fait du ski? – Jamais!*

Section 6 – Pronouns

Pronouns are the words we use to replace nouns, either when the person or thing we are talking or writing about is obvious, or when the noun or name has already been mentioned and it is unnecessary to repeat it.

There are six sets of pronouns in common use.

1. Subject pronouns

You will already be very familiar with eight of these pronouns, because they are the words we usually use to introduce verbs.

*je	I	nous	we
tu	you (friend)	vous	you (friends, stranger(s))
il	he or it	ils	they
elle	she or it	elles	they

*The pronouns *je* and *nous* are used by the person(s) speaking or writing.

The pronouns *tu* and *vous* are used to replace the name(s) of the person(s) being spoken or written to.

The pronouns *il, elle* and *ils, elles* are used to replace the name of the person(s) or thing(s) doing the action of the verb.

There is another, ninth subject pronoun called *on*. Literally, this is translated as 'one', but it is very useful to convey the idea of 'people', 'you' or 'we' when generalising.

e.g.

On doit payer ici.

One must pay here.
You have to pay here.
People must pay here.
We have got to pay here.

It can also be used to replace passive statements, such as:

A new school is being built.
On construit une nouvelle école.

or

It is said that the tunnel ...
On dit que le tunnel ...

You can see from the examples that *on* needs the same part of the verb as *il/elle*.

2. Reflexive pronouns

These are the pronouns we use to refer back to the subject or doer of the verb. They are:

me	myself	nous	ourselves
te	yourself	vous	yourselves, yourself
se	himself, herself, oneself, themselves		

Pronouns: direct object

We use them in such everyday statements as:
    Je m' appelle Martine.
    Ils s' appellent Yves et Luc.
and
    Je me lave à sept heures.
    On se lave dans la salle de bains.

Je me lave à sept heures

3. Object pronouns (direct)

These are the pronouns we use to replace the noun (whether it refers to person(s) or thing(s)) which goes on the end of the verb in English and is the person(s) or thing(s) being 'done' by the verb. There are three main object pronouns.

| *le*, him/it | *la*, her/it | *les*, them |

In English, the object pronoun follows the verb; in French, it <u>goes before it</u>.
    e.g. *Il achète les bonbons.*   He buys the sweets.
        Il les achète.   He buys them.

There are also object pronouns to refer to 'me', 'you', 'us'. For these, we use the same words as the reflexive pronouns 'myself', 'yourself/selves', 'ourselves'.

So: *Il me rencontre en ville.*   He meets me in town.
       Tu peux nous rendre
          visite dimanche.   You can visit us on Sunday.

Pronouns: indirect object, of place, partitive

4. Object pronouns (indirect)

These are the pronouns we use to mean 'to him', 'to her', 'to them', and to replace the noun which follows the verb in English to express to whom or for whom the verb is 'being done'. There are just two of these:

| *lui,* to him/to her | *leur,* to them |

In French, these pronouns go <u>in front of the verb.</u>
- e.g. *Je donnerai un disque <u>à mon frère.</u>* I'll give a record (to) my brother.
  Je <u>lui</u> donnerai un disque. I'll give <u>him</u> (=to him) a record.

5. The place pronoun (= there)

This is a single word used to replace a group of words (or a phrase) referring to a place or position. There is just one choice:

| *y,* there |

Like all other pronouns, it must go <u>before the verb</u> in French.
- e.g. *Il va <u>au collège</u> à pied.* He walks to school.
  Il <u>y</u> va à pied. He walks there.

Ils y vont à pied

6. The partitive pronoun (= of it, of them)

This is also a single word and it is used principally when we want to refer to a number or quantity of some thing(s) which we have already mentioned and don't want to repeat.

There is just one choice of pronoun:

| *en,* of it/of them |

- e.g. *Nous avons cinq chambres.*
  Il y <u>en</u> a trois au premier étage et il y <u>en</u> a deux au deuxième étage.
  Tu as combien <u>de frères</u> ? = J'<u>en</u> ai deux.

Section 7 – Idioms

You may never have heard of idioms, but you must certainly have used them – probably on your very first day of French!

So what are they?

When you ask someone *'Ça va bien?'* to say 'How are you?' or when you say *'J'ai douze ans'* to state your age, you are using idioms.

Idioms are easy, if you learn them by using them, as French people do. But if you have tried saying that your 'grandmother is better', or that your 'twin brothers are four' you may have found them not quite so easy.

The secret to using idioms correctly involves
    a) understanding what the structure actually means;
and b) being systematic.

Some of the commonest and most important idioms involve the Big Four verbs – to be, to have, to go, to do. We are going to concentrate on just three groups of idioms using *aller, avoir* and *faire*.

1. Being well/better

Instead of using parts of *être* (= to be), we must use parts of *aller* (= to go).

So, when you say . . .	it means something like . . .
Ça va bien?	Are 'things' going well?
Je vais bien.	I'm 'going' well.
Comment allez-vous?	How are you 'going'?

To talk about other people, and how they are, simply substitute the correct part of *aller* (to go) instead of 'to be'.

So, to say . . .	use . . .
My grandma isn't well.	*Ma grand-mère ne va pas bien.*
My sisters are well.	*Mes soeurs vont bien.*

If you want to talk about someone being better, change *bien* (= well) to *mieux* (= better), but still use part of *aller*.

So, to say . . .	use . . .
Thank you, I'm better.	*Merci, je vais mieux.*
My dad is better.	*Mon père va mieux.*

Idioms

2. Being ... years old, etc.

Being ... years old	*Avoir ... ans*
Being hungry	*Avoir faim*
Being thirsty	*Avoir soif*
Being frightened	*Avoir peur*
Being hot	*Avoir chaud*
Being cold	*Avoir froid*

If we want to express any of these ideas in English, we use the verb 'to be'.

e.g. My brother is ten (years old).
Are you hungry? I am thirsty.
My dog is frightened.
I am cold.

In French, all these ideas must be expressed by using parts of *avoir*.

So, when you say ...	it means something like ...
Mon frère a dix ans. *Tu as faim?* *Mon chien a peur.* *J'ai froid.*	My brother 'has' ten years. 'Have' you hunger? My dog 'has' fear. I 'have' cold.

To talk about any other people, and any of these ideas, don't fall into the trap of using the 'English' verb. You must be systematic and choose the correct part of *avoir*, not *être*.

So, to say ...	use ...
My sisters are four. We are thirsty. Are you frightened?	*Mes soeurs ont quatre ans.* *Nous avons soif.* *Tu as peur?*

If you want to use any of these expressions when you are talking or writing about the past or the future, be systematic in using *avoir* instead of the English 'to be'.

So, to say the past ...	use the past of *avoir* ...
I was thirsty. They were frightened.	*J'avais soif.* *Ils avaient peur.*

Idioms

To say the future . . .	use the future of *avoir* . . .
She <u>will be</u> eleven. You <u>will be</u> hungry!	*Elle <u>aura</u> onze ans.* *Tu <u>auras</u> faim!*

3. Going camping, etc.

Going camping	*Faire du camping*
Going ski-ing	*Faire du ski*
Going riding	*Faire de l'équitation*
Going for a walk	*Faire une promenade*
Going shopping	*Faire* { *les courses* / *des achats* }

In English, all these expressions use 'to go'. In French, you must avoid using *aller* 'to go'; instead you must use part of *faire* 'to do'.

So, to say . . .	use . . .
My brother <u>is going</u> for a walk. My parents <u>are going</u> shopping. We <u>go</u> camping.	*Mon frère <u>fait</u> une promenade.* *Mes parents <u>font</u> les courses.* *Nous <u>faisons</u> du camping.*

If you want to use any of these expressions in the past or the future, you must be systematic and use the correct part of *faire* instead of the English 'to go'.

So, to say the past . . .	use the past of *faire* . . .
We <u>went</u> for a walk. They <u>went</u> camping.	*Nous <u>avons fait</u> une promenade.* *Ils <u>ont fait</u> du camping.*

To say the future . . .	use the future of *faire* . . .
I <u>shall be going</u> riding. They <u>will go</u> ski-ing.	*Je <u>vais faire</u> de l'équitation.* *Ils <u>vont faire</u> du ski.*

Listening: shorter extracts

12 Skills Guide

Listening

Listening is a <u>passive</u> skill. This means that you simply have to recognise and understand the French being spoken on a tape played to you in the examination room.

There are usually two Listening Tests, one at Basic Level and one at Higher Level. For some Examination Boards, you do the Basic Listening on a different day from the Higher, on the pattern:

    Listen – Read – Write

on each day. For other boards, you do both levels of Listening Test on the same day, on a pattern such as:

    Basic   –   Basic   –   Higher   –   Higher
    Listening   Reading   Reading   Listening.

Whatever the format, the nature of the test is the same. You have a booklet giving questions in English, and you hear some short and some longer items of French, e.g. announcements, conversations, descriptions, etc. You hear these twice. The tape is spaced to give you time to study the English question and to write your answer <u>in English</u>. The spacing is generous, and you have plenty of time to write your answer if you know it! You do <u>not</u> have time to count through the days, months, numbers, etc. on your fingers if you don't know them!

You may write at any time during the test, not just in the gaps, and you do not need to write full sentence answers.

There are two types of listening – listening for detail, and listening for gist (general meaning).

Shorter extracts

In the shorter extracts of French, you will be asked to listen for just one or two details, such as a price and a time, or a platform number and a town. Usually (but not always), you will hear the details in the order of the questions.

For these shorter extracts, you should bear five points in mind:
- Read the question(s) before you hear the French.
- If you hear all the detail(s) you need at the first hearing, write your answers.
- Use the second hearing to check your answers.
- <u>Do not</u> spend time writing just one answer during the gap and continue writing into the second hearing, because you may miss the second answer.

Listening: longer extracts, hints

- If you hear just one of your answers the first time, write it quickly, or jot it in the margin, so that you can listen carefully for your other answer.

Longer extracts

When there are longer extracts of French, you will often need to understand the gist before you know where and when to listen for the details. In this case, it is essential to listen to the first hearing, making notes if you wish, before you decide on answers and fill them in. Keep your eye on the questions, and identify which bit of the conversation or description gives you which answer.

For longer extracts, at both levels, there are six points to remember:
- Read the questions before you hear the French.
- Keep looking at the questions and spotting answers as you listen.
- Jot down any numbers, days, etc., briefly, as you listen.
- Fill in any answers you know in the first gap, but read again the questions you haven't solved on the first hearing.
- <u>Listen</u> during the second hearing, and jot down any details as you hear them.
- Write your answers properly in the second gap – it is usually very long!

A few hints

1. The questions are often a useful clue. They tell you something about the French before you even hear it. Make the most of the clues you are given!

Make the most of the clues you are given

2. Check that you <u>do</u> answer what is asked. 'On Friday' does not answer 'Where did he go?'. Many candidates misread the question and then give the wrong answer.

3. Don't panic! You may only <u>need</u> to understand half the conversation to work out the answers. If you <u>can't</u> do a question, don't give up, keep listening. Later questions may be easier!

Speaking: rôle-play

🎞️ On side 2 of the tape accompanying this Grade Booster, there is a series of random items in French. Play the tape as many times as you wish and practise by answering the questions in English.

Speaking
Rôle-play

This is the part of the examination candidates tend to fear most, often unnecessarily.

You will be expected to perform (i.e. talk your way through) two, three, four or five rôle-plays.

Format

The format of the rôle-plays also varies according to the level and the Board. You may be asked to perform only structured rôles, where there are three, four, five or seven numbered items to be communicated in a set sequence; or a combination of structured and unstructured rôles, where you are given a situation and a task to be fulfilled, and the freedom to organise it in the way you want, or can.

Neither you nor your teacher/examiner has any choice of which rôles you are given. It is quite simply the luck of the draw.

There is likely to be one rôle you can't do (were absent for, didn't fit in, etc.) – or so you think when you first see it!

Here is some advice on how to tackle rôle-plays (easy or otherwise!).

Before the day

1. It is impossible to cover <u>every</u> possible rôle-play, but do work through as many different rôles as you can.
2. Many rôles are similar and phrases may be interchangeable. Collect such phrases and work out the variations.
3. Learn the basic key phrases. There are fifty in Appendix 1.

On the day

1. Don't panic! Keep calm!

If it looks impossible, there <u>will</u> be parts you can borrow from rôles you *can* do.

If it looks easy, make sure it <u>is</u> what you think. Many marks can be lost by misreading or seeing what you <u>want</u> to see.

2. Read the rubric (introduction) to the rôle carefully. It is normally in English and is meant to set the scene. *Think* your way into the rôle. Imagine you are there!

Speaking: structured rôle-plays

Are you in France (usually, but not always!), another French-speaking country (possibly!) or at home in Great Britain (occasionally!)? This can be important for addresses, prices, etc.

Are you the one asking for help or making requests, or giving help (i.e. using questions or giving instructions)?

Is the teacher or examiner playing an adult or a child, a stranger or a friend? Knowing this is vital for the choice of *vous* or *tu*!

3. Read the rôle itself. Is it structured (numbered items)? Or unstructured (general task)?

Structured rôle-plays

1. Look at each item. Often, in order to express exactly what you are required to say, the wording is far more complicated than the task!

e.g. 'Ask your friend if he or she is hungry' requires: *Tu as faim?*

'Find out whether there is a car-park available in the vicinity' requires: *Il y a un parking près d'ici?*

2. Do not attempt to <u>translate</u> the items. Work out the <u>idea</u> you have to convey, think of the French you know which can convey that idea, and put it to use.

e.g. 'Ask for some chips' could be:

Je voudrais des frites.
Donnez-moi des frites.
Une portion de frites, s'il vous plaît.

or even: *Vous avez des frites?*

Speaking: unstructured rôle-plays

'Find out when the castle is open' could be:
Quand est-ce que le château est ouvert?
Le château est ouvert quand?
*Le château est ouvert tous les jours?
or even: *Le château est fermé le week-end?*

*If you forget the question word, it is often possible to get the information by asking about <u>one</u> possibility.

3. If you are required to make a long statement or a complicated request, don't be afraid to break it down into shorter parts. This is often the natural thing to do, anyway.

    e.g. 'Explain that you have lost your large, blue suitcase at the station' requires: *J'ai perdu ma valise. C'est une grande valise bleue. Je l'ai perdue à la gare.*

J'ai perdu ma valise   *C'est une grande valise bleue*   *Je l'ai perdue à la gare*

4. If you are struggling, your teacher or examiner will usually help you to get from one item to another. If this can be done without supplying the French words you need, you may well not lose marks at all. If your teacher/examiner has to supply some of your part, you will lose some marks, but it may well be worth it to get on to a part you <u>can</u> do later on.

Unstructured rôle-plays

These <u>look</u> far more complicated than they are! They usually consist of a description of the task rather than a list of items, and a point to watch, such as: 'Make sure you get the <u>first</u> train tomorrow'; or 'Insist you get an appointment for today'. In this type of rôle-play, your teacher/examiner is instructed to be uncooperative (by recommending the <u>fastest</u> train, or offering an appointment for tomorrow, etc.) to test whether or not you can adjust and adapt your response.

Speaking: conversation

In unstructured rôles, it is essential to do five things:
- Study the rubric carefully, <u>think</u> yourself completely into the rôle – and <u>keep thinking</u>.
- Work out ways of communicating each element of your task. If no order is suggested, think of your best starting-point, but be ready for alternatives.
- Try to anticipate what problem will arise (e.g. item x sold out; no more size 39 in blue, etc.) and what to say to get what you need, etc.
- Keep the overall task in mind and make sure you don't forget any of the elements.
- Be prepared to argue if necessary. Don't be put off by your teacher/examiner, who is also playing a rôle.

Finally, remember that you are not being tested on your <u>acting</u>. However, if you are complaining, you should <u>sound</u> angry. If you are inviting someone to a party, you should <u>sound</u> enthusiastic.

Conversation

This part of the examination normally follows the rôle-plays and comes as a relief to most candidates. However, don't relax <u>too</u> much. Although it is meant to sound like a chat, there is a purpose behind most questions and you still need your wits about you!

Format

The format varies according to the Examination Board you are entered with.

You may be given the opportunity to nominate some of the topics you would prefer to discuss. Your teacher/examiner may then include one of your choices.

Alternatively, the Examination Board may decide which range of topics must be used for all candidates in each session.

How to tackle the conversation

You will normally have been working with your teacher/examiner for several months or years in preparation for this part of the examination. Whether you worked with him or her in practice situations on your own, answered questions as part of a full class, worked in a group or with a partner, or even sat and listened to others answering, makes no difference! You will know your teacher/examiner's voice and accent and the way in which he or she phrases questions and prompts you to talk in French about yourself, your friends and family, your routine and interests, and maybe even your opinions! This is a considerable

Speaking: conversation

advantage over the situation experienced by your older brothers and sisters or your parents, who had to face an unknown visiting examiner.

Before the day

- Make the most of this advantage by taking <u>every</u> opportunity to practise with your teacher/examiner.
- Look back through your books and highlight all the material (examples, answers, descriptions) you have worked on within each topic, which might be usable in another topic.
- Listen carefully to the way your teacher/examiner asks questions. If your teacher has known you for a long time, he or she may use *tu* to you (as in this Grade Booster); or your teacher may have started to use the more adult *vous*.
- Work through the topics and, as suggested in Chapters 1-10, prepare the material you need for yourself, your home, your family, etc., so that you are ready to respond to the questions. Do not learn a speech, as this is not acceptable and will not be marked.
- Make sure you are familiar with the different question words and the key time words (listed in Appendix, pages 119-20) so that you can recognise what is being asked.

On the day

- Listen to the questions carefully. Check what you are being asked by listening for those questions and key words. Do not assume that the questions will be in the order you learnt or prepared them.
- Listen to the questions for clues to help you answer. Check whether there is one verb-word (present tense) or two verb-words (probably past perfect or future with *aller*). Often you can convert the question into your answer.
- Listen for those questions which ask you to talk about (*raconter...*) or describe (*décrire...*), and take the opportunity to give longer answers – but <u>not</u> speeches.

*Give longer answers –
but* not *speeches*

Do not make life difficult for yourself by trying to give every minute detail accurately. This is not a recommendation to invent answers or tell lies – which can cause more difficulties than they avoid – but there are occasions when it might be easier to talk about alternative activities in which you are or were involved.

For instance, if you spent *hier soir* playing tiddly-winks with a half-cousin from Canada, it might be a good idea to talk about the tennis you played with your sister the night before!

Reading

Like listening, reading is a passive skill. Because of this, the range of vocabulary you are expected to recognise and understand is considerably wider than that which you are required to speak and write.

There are usually two Reading Tests, one at Basic Level and one at Higher. For some Examination Boards, the two tests will be on different days, following the Basic and Higher Listening Tests, but for other Boards you will do both tests on the same day. If this pattern is followed, you may be given both tests together and allowed to move on to the second test when you feel ready.

PACING or TIMING yourself is important in reading tests. Because the reading usually follows the listening, where the speed at which you must work is determined for you by the spaces on the tape, some candidates find it difficult to strike the correct balance, particularly if the two Reading Tests are together. Either they panic at the sight of so many pages and rush their answers, misreading, missing out and making careless mistakes, or they feel so relaxed because they don't have to answer during a set pause on a tape that they spend too much time trying to understand every word and do not finish all the questions. Either way, the results can be disastrous.

- Take sufficient time to read the question(s) carefully and the item a couple of times.
- Make sure you: give all the information required in each question; don't include information which has not been asked for in the question you are answering; write clearly and neatly, in English.

After about ten minutes, check your progress to see if you are on target to finish in time. If you have already finished after ten minutes, go back and check your answers against the passage. You must have missed something!

The items and passages vary considerably.

Reading: shorter items, longer items

For shorter items

1. Read the introduction carefully. It normally sets the scene by saying where you could find the sign. Then think about the situation and what you could expect.
2. Read the question itself. This usually gives even more help.
3. Now read the item. You will probably recognise at least half the French and can then try to work the rest out logically.

Sample question

Here is an exam question (LEAG, June 1988) where logical thinking can give you a lot of help:

You go to a French bank to change some money. You see this notice by the door. What is the first thing you must do to open the door?	**POUR ENTRER** 1 – SONNER 2 – ATTENDRE DECLIC 3 – POUSSER – ENTRER

You are told you are outside a bank. You will recognise *entrer* = to go in, and probably *attendre* = to wait. What must you do <u>before</u> you wait? It must be either knock or ring! You have a 50% chance of choosing the correct 'ring'.

For longer items

Don't be put off by longer items! Although they need more time because there is more to read, they also give more clues and the answer is less dependent on a single word.

Longer items <u>can</u> test reading for detail, but often they test reading for gist – general sense. Either way, you will need to look at the full extract, either to locate the detail or to get the gist.

For these items:
1. Read the rubric – it's just as helpful to know <u>what</u> you are reading.
2. Read the question – not to answer it at this stage, but to pick up clues and give you an idea of which key words to try to pin-point.
3. Read the whole item, or section, not just an odd line. Look for key words as you read.
4. If you are looking for details, make sure you look for them all – 'When?' may well need a day <u>and</u> a time which could be two or three lines apart.
5. If the question requires a general answer, don't be afraid to phrase it in your own words – don't translate the French word by word.

Reading: longer items

Sample question

Look at this question from an NEA 1989 exam paper:

Your friend Rebecca has received this letter from her pen-friend Nathalie:

Mercredi 10 Mai.

Chère Rebecca,

Comment vas-tu ? Moi, je vais bien. Ici, il fait beau. Je suis impatiente de te revoir.
Mon frère a son permis de conduire depuis la semaine dernière. C'est pratique pour moi qui sors souvent ! Maman et papa vont bien.
Ma cousine va se marier le mois prochain. Toute la famille sera là. Il y aura mon oncle, tu te souviens de lui ? Ma tante sera absente parce qu'elle a eu un accident et elle est à l'hôpital pour deux mois ! Mes grands-parents sont allés dans les Alpes, ce qui leur a fait du bien.
Je suis allée au cinéma avec mon petit ami, Jean-Luc. Nous avons vu "Crocodile Dundee II". C'était très amusant.
Bon, je dois y aller maintenant.

Amitiés.

Nathalie

Rebecca asks you for some help in understanding the letter.
She asks you what Nathalie says about:

(a) Her brother.

....

(b) Her parents.

....

(c) Her grandparents.

....

Writing: format

This is a longer item which is not really very difficult. For question (a) about Nathalie's brother, you need to look for the key word *frère*. You read that he has a *permis* – permission or permit for something – and he got it last week. You could guess *conduire* if you didn't know it – it isn't a fishing permit (no *pêche*), so it could be 'driving'. The next part of the sentence – *c'est pratique* – *je sors* – is meant as a further clue.

Question (b) about the girl's parents is equally easy to spot. *Maman et papa vont bien*. To answer, you need to know that this is the *ils* part of the idiom in line 1 *je vais bien*, 'I am well'. So, her parents are well.

For question (c), her grandparents went to the Alps <u>and</u> it did them good.

Don't panic!

- One final hint – don't panic when you see long passages of French. Look through them carefully till you spot the key words. As you can see, you don't <u>have</u> to understand every word.

Writing

Writing is the one skill which is not compulsory but it is preferable to include at least Basic Writing.

Some candidates feel nervous about writing in French because they find spelling, accents and endings difficult, but in fact writing is a fairer test than speaking, because it is based on a wider range of language and is less dependent on the luck of the draw. If you can <u>communicate</u> the required information in written French effectively, you will be scoring points. If you can do so by using a good range of vocabulary, and using verbs, genders and tenses accurately, you will be given extra credit to help you to achieve that higher grade. This book is designed to help you do just that!

Format

The type of task set varies (considerably) depending on the Examining Board, as does the amount of choice and format of the questions.

Writing: tackling the questions

1. At Basic Level, you may be asked to
   1 – Fill in a form.
   2 – Complete a letter or questionnaire by filling in gaps.
   3 – Write a message.
   4 – Write or reply to an invitation.
   5 – Write a postcard.
   6 – Write a short, informal letter.

At Higher Level, you might be asked to
   1 – Write a longer, informal letter.
   2 – Write a formal letter.
   3 – Write an account or a description.
   4 – Write a report or story.

2. The number of options varies. Some Boards give you two options for each question; some give you the choice of two out of three; others expect you to do both set questions.

If you do have a choice:
a) Make sure you follow the instructions precisely. Don't answer 1a and 1b when it should be 1a or 1b;
b) Take time to study the tasks and analyse what is required in each, and which will give you the better chance to display your skills.

Tackling the questions

Whatever the format and however wide or limited the choice, it is important to follow a few golden rules:

- Write what you know. Don't invent what you don't know.
- Write what is relevant to the question, not just everything you can think of under a particular topic.
- Make intelligent use of the language given in a model or letter to answer, but don't just copy! You *can* find considerable help with vocabulary, gender, verb structure, etc., if you look, think and adapt.
- Think yourself into the task. You may have to change sex, or nationality, to answer a particular question.
- Think about the nature of the task: are you asking, instructing or giving information? Are you writing
    about NOW (= present)
    or   EARLIER (= past)
    or   PLANS FOR LATER (= future)?
- Think about the style of the language. Is it clipped (as in a message), or chatty (as in a *tu* letter), or official (as in a formal *vous* letter)?

Writing: specific tasks

● Don't waste time working out your whole answer in full, then copying it out neatly. Instead <u>plan</u> the points you must make, list the verbs you need, work out the tenses, convert the *je* part to *nous* or *il* or whatever forms you may need.

Specific tasks

1. Form-filling

This is relatively easy, if you understand the headings. Read the whole form before you start, so that you don't put in too much information too soon. Check carefully whether you are to be yourself, and whether the address, etc., is to be in England or France. Often you will need to sign the form, and you may have to give the place and date of the signature. If you see

    a)_____ , *le* b)_____,

you need to put a suitable town (a) and a sensible date (b).

2. Gap-filling

This can vary in difficulty. Often it takes the form of an outline letter, and you are informed, in English, what is to go in the gaps. There is a great temptation simply to translate the English into French. But to answer the question well, you must ensure that the French you fill in fits the structure of the actual sentence:

    e.g. *Bonville est situé_____ de Grandvillon*
        Add 'ten kilometres from'
        Bonville est situé <u>à dix kilomètres</u> de Grandvillon.
    e.g. *Je suis restée quinze jours_____*
        Add 'with your friend Isabelle'
        Je suis restée quinze jours <u>chez mon amie Isabelle.</u>

Je suis restée quinze jours chez mon amie Isabelle

Writing: specific tasks

When you have filled all the gaps, it is important to check:
a) that you have the correct information in the correct gap;
b) that the finished text reads like French!

3. Writing messages, postcards and notes

As in English, you should use short sentences, or even sentences with odd words left out!

For example: Write a postcard to your French pen-friend's family, telling them when you arrived, where your hotel is, what it is like, where you spent yesterday, your plans for Saturday. You could say:

If you have a model or an item to answer, look very carefully for vocabulary and structures which will be relevant and can be adapted to your answer.

4. Writing informal letters

When writing informal letters, you should try to use full sentences, fitting in all the information required. This may be listed in the rubric or 'hidden' in a letter to be answered. Try to make your letter interesting, but not at the expense of the material you <u>must</u> communicate.

If a letter <u>is</u> supplied, make sure you answer as the 'right' person and use the help given.

    e.g. Given: *Tu <u>as reçu</u> beaucoup de cadeaux?*
        Response: *J'<u>ai reçu</u> une montre . . .*   (past tense)
        Given: *Après les examens je <u>vais partir</u> en vacances. Et toi?*
        Response: *Après mes examens je <u>vais</u> <u>travailler</u>*
                  dans le café.   (future)

Given: *Est-ce que tout le monde va bien?*
Response: *Je vais bien, mais mon frère a la grippe.* (idiom)

5. Writing formal letters

In this type of letter you are expected to be very factual, to use the correct format wherever possible, and to use *vous* for 'you'. Your course book should supply the formats.

For example, if you were set the task of writing to book hotel accommodation for your family of four, for a fortnight in August, with half-board, and enquiring whether there was a swimming-pool, you would need this type of letter:

Mrs. J. Jones
51, Heath Lane
Newton
Angleterre

                              Newton, le 15 mai 1992.

                              Hôtel Bellevue
                              Bonville
                              France

Monsieur,

Je voudrais passer (quinze jours avec ma famille) dans votre hôtel. Pouvez-vous me réserver (deux chambres – une chambre avec un lit à deux personnes et avec douche pour mon mari et moi, et une chambre à deux lits pour mes fils âgés de neuf et douze ans—pour les nuits du sept au vingt août, en demipension, si possible). Voudriez-vous m'indiquer le tarif (pour adultes et pour enfants, s'il vous plaît)? Je vous serais très reconnaissante de bien vouloir me dire s'il y a (une piscine près de l'hôtel).

Je vous prie d'agréer, Monsieur, l'expression de mes sentiments distingués.

Jane Jones

Writing: specific tasks

Je voudrais passer quinze jours avec ma famille dans votre hôtel

6. Writing an account, a report or a story, etc.

This is the type of task which often has a visual stimulus to support the rubric. You must read the rubric carefully and not just react to the visual material, which could set you off on the wrong track.

In this type of task, it is vital to make the right decision about the tense or tenses required, about whether you will be writing as *je* or *nous* or about *il* or *elle*, and about how you are going to link the given information to show off the French you know – and hide what you don't know.

Before you start writing your answer proper, make a list of the verbs you know which would be relevant. Use the spare paper, list them as infinitives or as *je* parts, ready to convert them where necessary. Verbs form the backbone of any account, and once you have established those, the who? what? where? when? will soon slot in.

    e.g. *je suis allé(e)*
         je suis parti(e)
         j'ai rencontré
         j'ai acheté → *il a acheté*
         j'ai mangé → *nous avons mangé*

Thus:
    Samedi dernier je <u>suis</u> <u>allé</u> en ville. Je <u>suis</u> <u>parti</u> à dix heures, et j'<u>ai</u> <u>rencontré</u> mon ami Jean-Luc devant la poste. J'<u>ai</u> <u>acheté</u> un pull noir, et Jean-Luc <u>a</u> <u>acheté</u> des cassettes. Nous <u>avons</u> <u>mangé</u> une pizza...

Writing: starters and finishers

Starters and finishers for cards or letters

1. Card

		Heading – town, day
Start	– *Salut!*	
Finish	– *A bientôt*	
You – (one person)	*tu*	Your – *ton/ta/tes*
You – (plural)	*vous*	Your – *votre/votre/vos*

2. Informal letter

Heading – town, date

Start – *Cher Philippe,/Chère Isabelle,/ Chers Philippe et Isabelle,*
Finish – *Amitiés,/Affectueusement,*

You – (one person) *tu*   Your – *ton/ta/tes*
You – (plural)   *vous*   Your – *votre/votre/vos*

3. Formal letter

Heading
Your address – top left
Their address – next right
Date – right, above their address

Start – *Monsieur,/Madame,/Messieurs,*
Finish – *Je vous prie d'agréer, Monsieur/Madame/Messieurs, l'expression de mes sentiments distingués.*

You – one person / plural   *vous*   Your – *votre/votre/vos*

Appendix 1

Question words

Où?
  Where?
Qui?
  Who?
Que?
  What?
Qu'est-ce que . . . ?
  What . . . ?
Quand?
  When?
Quel? Quelle?
  Which?
Comment?
  How?
Combien?
  How much?
A quelle heure?
  At what time?
De quelle couleur?
  What colour?
Pourquoi?
  Why?
Quoi?
  What?
  (after preposition)

To turn a statement into a question

Est-ce que . . . ?

Key phrases for rôle-play

Bonjour!
  Hello
Au revoir!
  Goodbye
Salut!
  Hi!
A bientôt!
  See you soon!
Bonne nuit!
  Goodnight
S'il vous (te) plaît
  Please
Merci
  Thank you
Pardon!
  Excuse me
Je regrette
  I'm sorry
**Je vous en prie
(Je t'en prie)**
  It's a pleasure
Je ne comprends pas
  I don't understand
Voulez-vous répéter . . . ?
  Will you repeat . . . ?
Comment dit-on . . . en français?
  What is . . . in French?
Bon appétit!
  Enjoy your meal
Ça va bien
  I'm fine
Je voudrais . . .
  I'd like . . .
Donnez-moi . . .
  Give me . . .
Avez-vous . . . ?
  Do you have . . .
  Have you . . .
Voulez-vous . . . ?
  Will you . . . ?
C'est combien?
  How much does it cost?
Ça fait combien?
  How much does it come to?
C'est gratuit?
  Is it free of charge?
C'est libre?
  Is it vacant?
C'est tout?
  That's all?
C'est compris?
  Is it included?
Où se trouve . . . ?
  Where is . . . ?
Pour aller { **à . . . ?**
              au . . . ?
  How do I get to . . . ?
C'est loin?
  Is it far?
C'est fermé/ouvert?
  Is it closed/open?
J'ai faim/soif
  I'm hungry/thirsty
J'ai mal à . . .
  My . . . hurts! (any one!)
Je suis Anglais(e)
  I'm English
Je suis Écossais(e)
  I'm Scottish
J'aime . . .
  I like, love . . .
Je déteste . . .
  I hate . . .
(Est-ce que) je peux . . . ?
  May I . . . ?
J'ai perdu . . .
  I've lost . . .
Savez-vous . . . ?
  Do you know . . . ?
Pouvez-vous . . . ?
  Can you . . . ?
**C'est trop cher
(grand)**
  It's too expensive
  (large)
Ça ne marche pas
  It won't work
. . . est en panne
  . . . has broken down
C'est quel quai?
  Which platform?
C'est quelle ligne?
  Which route?

Expressions of time

... part à quelle heure?
What time does ... leave?
... arrive à quelle heure?
What time does ... arrive?
(Est-ce qu')il y a { un ...? / une ...?
Is there a ...?
Près d'ici
Near here
... commence à quelle heure?
When does ... start?
... finit à quelle heure?
When does ... finish?
Vous avez de la place?
Have you any room?
... par personne
... per person
J'ai besoin de ...
I need ...

Important expressions of time
aujourd'hui
today
hier
yesterday
avant-hier
day before yesterday
demain
tomorrow
après-demain
day after tomorrow
le matin
in the/a morning
l'après-midi (m)
in the/an afternoon
le soir
in the/an afternoon
pendant la nuit
in the night
ce matin
this morning
cet après-midi (m)
this afternoon
ce soir
this evening
hier soir
yesterday evening
demain matin
tomorrow morning
lundi
on Monday
samedi
on Saturday
le lundi
on a Monday
le samedi
on a Saturday
le week-end
at the weekend
samedi matin
Saturday morning
samedi soir
Saturday evening
dimanche dernier
last Sunday
dimanche prochain
next Sunday
la semaine dernière
last week
la semaine prochaine
next week
en été
in summer
en hiver
in winter
en juillet
in July
en janvier
in January
pendant les grandes vacances
during the summer holidays
pendant les vacances de Noël
during Christmas half-term
pendant les vacances de Pâques
during Easter half-term
pendant les vacances d'automne
during October half-term
d'abord
first of all
ensuite
next
alors
then, well
puis
then
enfin
finally
d'habitude
usually
quelquefois
sometimes
souvent
often
toujours
always
il y a trois jours
three days ago
il y a quatre ans
four years ago
depuis cinq ans
for five years
(in set phrases only)

Appendix 2

Cardinal numbers (one, two, three . . .)

To help you, numbers 1-100 are listed on the tape, after Chapter 10.

1-20
Know these! (how they sound and how to spell them).

un (une)	onze
deux	douze
trois	treize
quatre	quatorze
cinq	quinze
six	seize
sept	dix-sept
huit	dix-huit
neuf	dix-neuf
dix	vingt

21-60
Recognise these (quickly) and know the ones you need!

vingt et un(e)
vingt-deux
vingt-trois
etc.

trente
trente et un(e)
trente-deux
trente-trois
etc.

quarante
quarante et un(e)
quarante-deux
quarante-trois
etc.

cinquante
cinquante et un(e)
cinquante-deux
cinquante-trois
etc.

soixante

61-100
Because there is no single word in French for 70, 80 and 90, these numbers need special care.

You'll need to recognise them, <u>and</u> know the ones you need. They're easier to remember if you understand <u>how</u> they're made up! Initially, they are easy, following the previous pattern. So:

soixante et un(e)
soixante-deux
soixante-trois
soixante-quatre
soixante-cinq
soixante-six
soixante-sept
soixante-huit
soixante-neuf

<u>But then,</u> because there is no 'new' number for 70, keep adding on to 60 . . .

70 <u>*soixante-dix*</u> (= 60-10)
This pattern continues –
soixante et onze
soixante-douze
soixante-treize
soixante-quatorze
soixante-quinze
soixante-seize
soixante-dix-sept
soixante-dix-huit
soixante-dix-neuf

<u>But then,</u> because there is no 'new' number for 80, you have to follow a new pattern, based on 20s . . .

80 <u>*quatre-vingts*</u> (= 4 × 20) (or 4-20s)
So:
quatre-vingt-un(e)
quatre-vingt-deux
quatre-vingt-trois
quatre-vingt-quatre
quatre-vingt-cinq
quatre-vingt-six
quatre-vingt-sept
quatre-vingt-huit
quatre-vingt-neuf

And:
90 <u>*quatre-vingt-dix*</u>
quatre-vingt-onze (4-20s-11)
quatre-vingt-douze
quatre-vingt-treize
quatre-vingt-quatorze
quatre-vingt-quinze
quatre-vingt-seize
quatre-vingt-dix-sept
quatre-vingt-dix-huit
quatre-vingt-dix-neuf

And:
100 <u>*cent*</u>
Then you combine to make:
cent un(e)
cent deux
etc.
But:
deux cents
deux cent cinquante
deux cent cinquante-trois, etc.
and: *mille un(e)*
deux mille
deux mille cinq cents,
etc.

Cardinal numbers

When you will need cardinal numbers

1. Listening

This is the most important time. You will need to recognise numbers in: prices, times, ages, bus routes, platforms, addresses, etc. Use your common sense to work out what range of numbers is likely:

- Platforms are unlikely to go beyond twenty.

- Ages of brothers or sisters are probably under twenty, ages of adults and parents thirty to forty, of grandparents fifty-five plus.

- Prices are often in whole francs, or fifties or fives.

- Listen to where the word *francs* comes.
  Thus:
  deux cent cinquante francs = 250 F
  but:
  deux cents francs cinquante = 200,50 F
  And:
  vingt-cinq francs = 25 F
  but:
  vingt-francs cinq = 20,05 F

- Times will not go beyond fifty-nine (minutes) and twenty-three (hours) and will often be in multiples of five. Again watch the order of words.
  Thus:
  vingt-deux heures = 22 hours = 10 p.m.
  but:
  deux heures vingt = 2.20 a.m./p.m.

2. Speaking

In the conversation section, you are in control of the numbers you say. Make sure you have worked out the numbers you need for your family's ages, your own current age, your date of birth, address, number of pupils in school, etc.!

In the rôle-play section, you could need any number! But you have preparation time and can think it out. For this, you must know how to say one to twenty, the key numbers plus the system!

3. Reading

This should be the easiest part. It is normal only to write numbers in words up to about twenty, so you just need to recognise the spelling of those few. If you are required to answer with a number already written in figures, it will be to test if you understand the French that goes with that number (i.e. the food at that price on the menu, what happens at a certain time, etc.).

4. Writing

As in reading, you will not normally be expected to write in words numbers over twenty. Learn the basic twenty, plus simple dates. Don't forget to use the plural noun if you are writing more than one.
e.g. *J'ai trois frères*.
  Il y a 25 élèves dans ma classe.

Listening, Speaking, Reading and Writing

- See page 127 on how to learn numbers.

Ordinal numbers (first, second, third . . .)

In theory, there are as many ordinal numbers as there are cardinal ones, but in practice, you will need very few of the ordinal numbers.

There are just two special words: *premier* (*première*) for 'first', and *second* (*seconde*) as an alternative for 'second'.

All other ordinal numbers can be made up by adding the ending *-ième* to the basic (cardinal) number.

2nd = *deuxième* (more usual than *second(e)*)
3rd = *troisième*
4th = *quatrième* (omit the *e* of *quatre*)
5th = *cinquième* ⎱ NB: note spelling
9th = *neuvième* ⎰ of *cinquième* and *neuvième* etc.
10th = *dixième*
21st = *vingt et unième* (no connection with *premier*)

Ordinal numbers are used in such patterns as:
Prenez la quatrième rue à droite.
Mon appartement se trouve au troisième étage.
Le rayon des chaussures se trouve au cinquième étage.
C'est la troisième fois que je vais en France.
C'est son cinquième anniversaire.
etc.

Dates involving ordinal numbers

In English, we use ordinal numbers (fifth, twenty-first, etc.) to express the date. In French, you use only one ordinal number as a date – first.
So: *le premier janvier*
le premier avril
etc.
All other dates are expressed by using the basic, cardinal numbers.
So: *le quatre juin*
le quinze juillet
le vingt-cinq novembre
le trente et un décembre
etc.

When writing letters, it is safer to write *premier* as a word. Other short dates may be written in full, but long dates are normally written with figures.

e.g. *Je voudrais réserver le chambre pour une semaine, du 25 mai jusqu'au premier juin.*
Nous arriverons le cinq juillet et partirons le dix juillet.

To quote the year, begin *mille neuf cent . . .*

e.g. *Il est né le huit septembre mille* (or *mil*) *neuf cent soixante-dix-neuf* (8.9.1979)

Work out and learn your own date of birth –
Je suis né(e) le (on the) . . .

Appendix 3

Time

Using either digital time or clock-face time, you may need to ask or talk about:

a) what the time is

> *Quelle heure est-il?*
> *Il est . . . heures*, etc.

b) at what time something happens

> *A quelle heure . . . ?*
> *. . . à . . . heures*, etc.

1. Digital time

This is the kind of time shown on modern watches, airport and station clocks, video displays, etc. It consists of a display of three or four figures to indicate hours and minutes, and may be based on the twelve or twenty-four hour system.

To express digital time in French, you need numbers to twenty-four for the hours and fifty-nine for the minutes.

- If you are dealing with whole hours, you simply read off the figures, and add *heure(s)*.

So: **4:00** = *quatre heures*

and: **17:00** = *dix-sept heures*

but: **1:00** = *une heure*.

- If you are dealing with hours and minutes, you simply add the minutes on the end.

So: **4:15** = *quatre heures quinze*

and: **17:23** = *dix-sept heures vingt-trois*

- At midday **12:00**

you would use *douze heures*; and at midnight

24:00 or **0:00**

vingt-quatre heures.

- If you had to include a time in a piece of writing you would put:
  4.15 heures

2. Clock-face time

This is exactly what its name suggests, and is still the preferable type of time to use in informal conversation. It is only based on the twelve-hour system.

To express clock-face time, you will need numbers to twelve for the hours and up to twenty-nine for the minutes, plus phrases for half, quarter, to and past.

- If you are dealing with whole hours, you use exactly the same system as for the first twelve hours of digital time.

So:

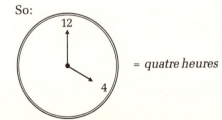

= *quatre heures*

Time

but:

= *une heure*

In addition:

= *midi*

and:

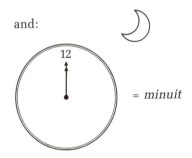

= *minuit*

● If you are dealing with hours and parts of hours, you need to add:
et quart, quarter past
et demie, half past
<u>moins</u> le quart, quarter to.

So:

= *deux heures et demie**

*But note: *midi et dem<u>i</u>*
minuit et dem<u>i</u>

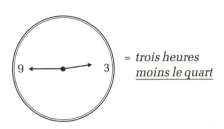

= *trois heures <u>moins le quart</u>*

● If you are dealing with hours and minutes, you need to add:

cinq	five past
dix	ten past
vingt	twenty past
vingt-cinq	twenty-five past

and:

moins cinq	five to
moins dix	ten to
moins vingt	twenty to
moins vingt-cinq	twenty-five to.

So:

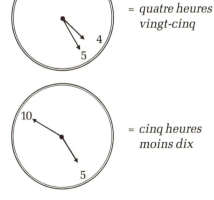

= *quatre heures vingt-cinq*

= *cinq heures moins dix*

● Practice in recognition is provided on the tape, after Chapter 10.

Appendix 4

In any language, there are two types of vocabulary: active and passive.

Passive vocabulary

Passive vocabulary is a collection of words (often more unusual than the active) which you are expected to <u>recognise and understand</u>, but not necessarily to use.

Wherever items of passive vocabulary occur, they are made more understandable by their context – that is, the type of situation in which they are used.

You are not expected to <u>learn</u> passive vocabulary. The more you listen and read, the more words you will recognise, but the key to understanding is <u>common sense</u> – working out what a word is likely to mean from the context in which it is used.

Active vocabulary

Active vocabulary is the collection of words in regular use which you are expected to <u>know</u>. You will need to be able to think of these words and use them in the various sections of the Speaking and Writing Tests.

In an ideal world, no one would need to <u>learn</u> vocabulary: you would come to know it naturally through hearing and seeing it, then using it, just as you do with your own, native language. To learn a foreign language, we usually have to speed the process up and at times learn <u>unnaturally</u>.

Have you found the method of learning which works best for you?

One thing is certain: sitting with your exercise book, vocabulary book, or worse still, the Syllabus vocabulary list, gazing at pages of random words, is a very ineffective way of learning. It is much more effective to break the process down into simple stages.

How to learn vocabulary

<u>Stage 1 – Collecting and sorting</u>

The first thing to do is to go through all your notebooks, collecting <u>groups</u> of words and re-listing them <u>together</u>. This in itself will help you to remember. Obvious groups would be: relatives, jobs, rooms, furniture, clothes, buildings, countryside, foods, drinks, presents, etc., etc. Less obvious are such things as: time phrases, weather, methods of travel, leisure verbs, routine verbs, etc.

How you arrange these groups of words may vary: you can use separate pages in a file, small pieces of card in envelopes, or self-adhesive notes which you can display group by group on a mirror or wall (some students even label the furniture itself!) whilst you learn. Whichever method you adopt, it must be easily expandable so that you can add words as you come across them. With lists, the meaning is best alongside; with cards or notes, it is best on the reverse.

- Whilst the use of *le* or *la* will not normally affect <u>communication</u>, using gender accurately will help to boost your grade. Many students find it helpful to list nouns in two colours.
- Students with a visual memory may prefer to list masculine nouns down one side of the page and feminine down the other!

Stage 2 – Repeating

The more times the vocabulary passes through your brain, the better you will know it. This is why gazing at it does so little good. Make yourself do something active to repeat the words.

- You could copy the French word, think of the English and write that.
- You could cover up the French and try writing it from memory (just looking at the English).
- You could say it semi-loud to yourself, covering up the French and thinking of it from the English and then the other way round.
- You could record it on to cassette, first French and English together, then just French (for you to answer in English), then just English, etc.

Stage 3 – Testing

This is the final stage and should not be tackled until you feel you know a large proportion of the vocabulary group you are working on. If you are tested too soon, you will only succeed in depressing yourself and want to give up. The tester can be a friend or relative, preferably someone who knows some French, but this is not essential. Questions may be:
'What is the French for . . . ?'
or 'Tell me ten items of clothing'
or 'A fruit beginning with 'A'' etc.

Crosswords, word-searches and quizzes (based on TV versions) are an excellent form of testing, if they are available – and they are fun to do.

How to learn numbers

To be successful, you must be able to translate numbers instantly. It is not enough to be able to chant them in order. In a Speaking Test, it causes an agonising wait if you have to mouth or finger-count all the way to sixteen or thirty-eight, and in a Listening Test, the tape will have moved on before you have worked it out.

Some Hints

First, work out (underline or highlight) the numbers from the lists which you will need. Then go through the sentences you will need and learn the numbers with them.
e.g. 62 = *soixante-deux*
   Mon grand-père a soixante-deux ans.

Then, tackle the rest – in groups first. Try the card method (100 bits of cards, figure on one side, word on the other); or the folded paper method (list – best in random order – with figures on left of fold, words on right).

Try reading or chanting –
   first forwards,
   then backwards,
   then odds,
   then evens.

- Make sure you have 'random recall' for numbers, i.e. you can think of them in any order.

Appendix 5

Practising interviews

In order to help you prepare for the conversation section with a friend or relative, one of the topics has been set out as a question and answers exercise.

The questions are based on those in the Topic chapter and follow the *tu* form.

There is an introductory question, followed by a choice: either one or two general questions or a few more specific questions. Your partner may ask you the questions in the set or varied order. You must recognise the question and respond with the most appropriate answer – starters are supplied.

Why not go through each Topic (here and in your notebooks) and make up your own interview practice sheets.

HOUSE/HOME

Où habites-tu?
Tu peux décrire ta maison/ta chambre?
Ta maison se trouve au centre-ville?
Ta maison est petite?
Il y a combien d'étages?
Et combien de pièces est-ce qu'il y a?
Quelles sont les pièces?
Qu'est-ce qu'il y a au rez-de-chaussée?
Où se trouve ta chambre?
Comment est ta chambre?
Qu'est-ce qu'il y a dans ta chambre?
Depuis quand est-ce que tu habites là?

FOLD

J'habite (à) _____

Oui, _____

Non, ma maison est située _____

Non, elle est _____

Il y (en) a _____

Il y a _____ pièces

(Ce sont) _____

Il y a _____

Elle se trouve _____

Elle est _____

Il y a _____

J'habite _____ depuis _____ ans